Holiday

A Comedy in Three Acts

by Philip Barry

A SAMUEL FRENCH ACTING EDITION

SAMUEL FRENCH

FOUNDED 1830

New York Hollywood London Toronto

SAMUELFRENCH.COM

ISBN   978-0-573-61019-6   Printed   in   U.S.A.   #10115

MUSIC USE NOTE

**IMPORTANT BILLING AND CREDIT
REQUIREMENTS**

Copy of original program of "HOLIDAY" as produced at The Plymouth Theatre, New York:

ARTHUR HOPKINS

Presents

HOLIDAY

A Comedy in Three Acts

By

PHILIP BARRY

Staged by Mr. Hopkins

Settings by Robert Edmond Jones

CAST OF CHARACTERS

LINDA SETON .... *Hope Williams*
JOHNNY CASE .... *Ben Smith*
JULIA SETON .... *Dorothy Tree*
NED SETON .... *Monroe Owsley*
SUSAN POTTER .... *Barbara White*
NICK POTTER .... *Donald Ogden Stewart*
EDWARD SETON .... *Walter Walker*
LAURA CRAM .... *Rosalie Norman*
SETON CRAM .... *Thaddeus Clancy*
HENRY .... *Cameron Clemens*
CHARLES .... *J. Ascher Smith*
DELIA .... *Beatrice Ames*

SCENES

ACT I. *Room on the Third Floor of* EDWARD SETON'S *House in New York.*
ACT II. *Room on the Top Floor.*
ACT III. *Room on the Third Floor.*

DESCRIPTION OF CHARACTERS

LINDA SETON: *She is twenty-seven, and looks about twenty-two. She is slim, rather boyish, exceedingly fresh. She is smart, she is pretty, but beside* JULIA'S *grace,* JULIA'S *beauty, she seems a trifle gauche, and almost plain.*

JOHNNY CASE: *Is thirty, medium-tall, slight, attractive-looking, luckily not quite handsome.*

JULIA SETON *is twenty-eight, and quite beautiful.*

NED SETON: *He is twenty-six. He is as handsome in his way as* JULIA *is in hers. His features are fine, a little too fine. He displaces very little, but no one minds: he is a nice boy.*

SUSAN: *Is thirty, smart and attractive.*

NICK POTTER: *He is about thirty-four, with an attractive, amusing face.*

EDWARD SETON: *He is fifty-eight, large, nervous, distinguished.*

LAURA: SETON'S *wife, is thirty-two, a shade taller than* SETON, *with a rather handsome, rather disagreeable face. She is as smartly dressed as a poor figure will allow.*

SETON CRAM: *He is thirty-six, somewhat bald, inclined to a waistline, but well turned out.*

HENRY: *He is fifty, of pleasant appearance, of pleasant manner.*

CHARLES: *A younger man-servant.*

DELIA: *A housemaid of about thirty-five.*

HOLIDAY

ACT ONE

SCENE: *A room on the third floor of* EDWARD
SETON'S *house in New York. The only entrance is at Left. It is a very large rectangular
room of the Stanford White period. The pan-
elling is heavy, the mouldings are heavy, the
three long windows looking out over the park
at Back are hung with heavy curtains. The
portrait of* SETON'S *father, by a contemporary
English master, hangs over the fireplace, at the
right. It is a handsome room, and quite a comfortable room, but rich, very rich. At Right
and Left are two comfortable sofas, a table behind each. On one table are two telephones, one
for the house, the second for outside. On the
other table, magazines and newspaper, and a
cigarette-box. This side of the sofa, near Center, are two upholstered benches, and at Right
and Left of each a large chair. In the corners
of the room, at Back, stand two more chairs, a
table and lamp beside each.*

TIME: *It is about twelve o'clock on a bright, cold
Sunday morning in mid-December, this year.*

AT RISE: *A fire is burning in the fireplace. Sunday*

papers are strewn upon a low table and beside a chair near it.

    JULIA SETON *is seated at a desk, Right, writing a note. She is twenty-eight, and quite beautiful. She writes in silence for a few minutes, then calls, in response to a knock at the door:*

JULIA. Yes? (HENRY *enters from Left.* HENRY *is the butler. He is fifty, of pleasant appearance, of pleasant manner.*) Oh, hello, Henry. How have you been? *(She seals the note.)*

HENRY. Well, thank you, Miss. We're very glad to have you back again.

JULIA. It was a lovely trip.

HENRY. A Mr. Case to see you, Miss. He said you expected him, so Charles is bringing him up.

JULIA. That's right. How many are we for lunch?

HENRY. Six, I believe. Only Mr. and Mrs. Cram are expected.

JULIA. Hasn't Miss Linda friends, too?

HENRY. Not as we've been told, Miss.

JULIA. Have an extra place set, will you?

HENRY. Yes, Miss. (HENRY *collects the newspapers from the floor and chairs, and piles them in a neat pile upon a table. After a moment* CHARLES, *a younger man-servant, appears in the doorway.*)

CHARLES. Mr. Case, Miss.

JULIA. *(Rises from the desk and calls in the direction of the hall)* Come in, Johnny! Quick!—Of all slow people. (CHARLES *stands aside to admit* JOHNNY CASE, *and enters after him.* JOHNNY *is thirty, medium-tall, slight, attractive-looking, luckily not quite handsome. He goes at once to* JULIA.)

JOHNNY. There was a traffic-jam. Men were dying like flies.—Did you really go to church?

JULIA. Yes, but I ducked the sermon. I was sure you'd get here before me. You're staying for **lunch, you** know.

JOHNNY. Thanks, I'd love to. (BOTH *look warily at the* TWO MEN *tidying up the room.)* I'm actually hungry again. Those same old shooting-pains.

JULIA. Isn't it extraordinary the appetite that place gives you? You should have seen the breakfast I ate on the train.

JOHNNY. Why wouldn't you join me? You were invited.

JULIA. Miss Talcott would have swooned away. She's the world's worriedest chaperon as it is. (HENRY *goes out.* CHARLES *has begun to gather ashtrays upon a larger tray.)* —You can leave the trays till later, Charles.

CHARLES. Very well, Miss. (*He moves toward the door.* JULIA *talks against his exit.)*

JULIA. *(To* JOHNNY*)* Have you ever known such cold?

JOHNNY. Never.

JULIA. It's hard to believe it was twenty degrees lower at Placid.

JOHNNY. You don't feel it, there.

JULIA. That's what they say.—And you can close the door, Charles. It makes a draught.

CHARLES. Yes, Miss.

JULIA. When Mr. Seton comes in, would you ring this room from the door? Two short ones.

CHARLES. Very good, Miss. (*He goes out, closing the door after him. For a moment* JULIA *and* JOHNNY *stand transfixed, looking at each other. Then* JULIA *smiles slightly and says:)*

JULIA. Hello, Sweet—— (*In an instant* JOHNNY *is beside her and she is in his arms, being kissed. At length she stands off from him, murmuring)* Johnny —Johnny—mind your manners.

JOHNNY. But dear, where are we?

JULIA. We're here, all right. (JOHNNY *moves away from her and looks about him.)*

JOHNNY. But where's "here"?

JULIA. Where I live. Don't you like it?

JOHNNY. But Julia, seriously, what *is* all this?

JULIA. All what?

JOHNNY. All this house—and armies of men underfoot picking up newspapers, and——

JULIA. Aren't you silly, Johnny. I told you where I lived. *(She seats herself upon a sofa)* —I wrote it on the back of an envelope for you.

JOHNNY. But it's enormous. I'm overcome. It's the Grand Central. How can you stand it?

JULIA. I seem to manage.

JOHNNY. Don't you find you rattle around a good deal in it?

JULIA. I hadn't noticed that I did.

JOHNNY. *(Cups his hands and calls through them)* Hoo! *(Then)* There's a bad echo.

JULIA. You stop criticizing this house, or I'll call the bouncer.

JOHNNY. But you must all be so *rich*, Julia!

JULIA. Well, we aren't poor.

JOHNNY. You should have told me, you really should.

JULIA. Would it have made any difference?

JOHNNY. *(Laughs)* Lord, yes! I'd have asked you to marry me in two days, instead of ten.

JULIA. *(A pause. Then)* How do you mean?

JOHNNY. I went through an awful struggle. You've no idea. I had very definite plans for the next few years, and at first a wife looked like quite a complication.

JULIA. What were the plans?

JOHNNY. For one thing, I was worried about having enough for both of us. If I'd known, I'd have spared myself. It's simply swell now. Good Julia.

JULIA. Aren't you funny, Johnny.

JOHNNY. Why?

JULIA. To talk about it.

JOHNNY. It? Money? Why? Is it so sacred?

JULIA. Of course not. But——

JOHNNY. I'm simply delighted, that's all.

JULIA. —That I have—uh—money?

JOHNNY. Yes. Sure. *(She laughs.)*

JULIA. You're amazing.

JOHNNY. But why not?—If I'd suddenly discovered you could play the piano I'd be delighted, wouldn't I?

JULIA. Is it like knowing how to play the piano?

JOHNNY. Well, they're both very pleasant accomplishments in a girl.

JULIA. But, my dear, you're going to make millions, yourself!

JOHNNY. Oh, no, I'm not.

JULIA. You are too!

JOHNNY. —Am not.

JULIA. Are too. *(A brief pause.)*

JOHNNY. How did you happen to decide I'd do, Julia?

JULIA. I fell in love with you, silly.

JOHNNY. You might have done that, and still not have wanted to marry me.

JULIA. I do, though.

JOHNNY. You know awfully little about me.

JULIA. *I* know enough.—You aren't trying to get out of anything, are you, Johnny?

JOHNNY. Watch me.

JULIA. Because you haven't a chance, you know. *(She rises and goes to the window at Back.)*

JOHNNY. But what's there different about me? What did it?

JULIA. You're utterly, utterly different.

JOHNNY. —I am a man of the pee-pul——

JULIA. That might be one reason.

JOHNNY. I began life with these two bare hands.

JULIA. —So did the gentleman over the fireplace.

(JOHNNY *looks at the portrait above the mantel.*)
—Take heart from Grandfather.

JOHNNY. You wouldn't tell me you're *those*
Setons!

JULIA. Forgive us, Johnny, but we are.

JOHNNY. *(Overwhelmed, lowers his head)* It's
too much.

JULIA. *(Lightly)* —What man has done, man
can do—or words to that effect. *(She is looking out
the window, down into the street.)*

JOHNNY. See here, child—if you think I'm a bud-
ding young Captain of Industry, or——

JULIA. Sh—wait a minute.

JOHNNY. What's the matter?

JULIA. It's the motor. At least I think—yes, it is.

JOHNNY. Him?

JULIA. Wait a minute—— No—it's only Linda.
Father must have decided to walk home with Ned.

JOHNNY. Did you tell him, as you planned to?

JULIA. *(Again moves toward the sofa)* Father?
Just exactly as I planned to.

JOHNNY. I'm still not sure that church was a good
place.

JULIA. I wanted to give him a chance to think, before he started talking. He never talks in church.

JOHNNY. What did you say?

JULIA. I said, "Look here, Father: I'm going to
marry Johnny Case." And he said, "What's that?"
And I said, "I said, I'm going to marry Johnny
Case."

JOHNNY. And he never even peeped?

JULIA. Oh, yes.—"And who may Johnny Chase
be?" "Case," I said. "Not Chase." "Well, Case,
then?"—I told him I'd met you at Placid, that he'd
meet you at luncheon and that you were with Sloan,
Hobson, Hunt and Sloan.—That was right, wasn't
it?

JOHNNY. Sloan, Hobson, *Hunter* and Sloan.

JULIA. It was near enough. He said, "I know Sam Hobson," and began to pray rapidly—and that was all there was to it.

JOHNNY. But probably there'll be more.

JULIA. Yes, probably a lot more—I hope you're feeling strong. *(They seat themselves together upon the sofa at Right.)*

JOHNNY. Seriously, how do you think he'll take it?

JULIA. *(Laughs)* —Seriously! *(Then)* You'll have one big thing in your favor, Johnny.

JOHNNY. What?

JULIA. You'll see.

JOHNNY. I know: It's this necktie.

JULIA. Johnny——

JOHNNY. Julia——

JULIA. Don't jest, boy.

JOHNNY. Oh, darling, let's not let the fun go out of it!

JULIA. Is it likely to?

JOHNNY. No, but——

JULIA. Say it.

JOHNNY. What was the point of spilling it so quickly?

JULIA. I had to tell Father. It would be different if Mother were alive. I could have broken it gently through her, I suppose. But as it is——

JOHNNY. —Eventually, I know. But why the rush?

JULIA. I had to tell him. He'd never have forgiven me.

JOHNNY. It could have been such a swell guilty secret for awhile.

JULIA. I can't see what particular fun a secret would have been.

JOHNNY. Can't you, dear?

JULIA. No.

JOHNNY. All right.

JULIA. Oh, don't say "all right" that way! You don't mean "all right."

JOHNNY. *(Smiles)* All right.

JULIA. You're the most outspoken, direct man I've ever known, and you sit there, sobbing over—

JOHNNY. It's all right, dear. Really it is.

JULIA. I thought you wanted us to be married as soon as possible.

JOHNNY. I do.

JULIA. Well, then.

JOHNNY. When shall we?

JULIA. There's another place Father comes in.

JOHNNY. I should think it would be pretty much up to you.

JULIA. You don't know Father.

JOHNNY. But let's not have an elaborate one— wedding, I mean.

JULIA. I doubt if we can avoid it. We've got to think of Father.

JOHNNY. It's getting pretty complicated.

JULIA. You didn't think it would be simple, did you?

JOHNNY. I suppose I just didn't think.

JULIA. You couldn't have. *(In sudden exasperation)* Oh, Johnny, *Johnny*—what's the matter with you?

JOHNNY. I just hate the thought of sitting down with a man and being practical about you—so soon, I mean. (JULIA *softens.*)

JULIA. —Angel. *(She kisses him, lightly)* It's got to be done, though.

JOHNNY. All right. I'll gird up my loins.—You know, I'll bet he'll hate this necktie. It doesn't look substantial.

JULIA. You might sit like this—covering it with your hand.

JOHNNY. I love you, Julia.

JULIA. I love you, Johnny.

JOHNNY. That's the main thing, isn't it?

JULIA. Darling, that's everything——

JOHNNY. Kiss?

JULIA. With pleasure—— *(They kiss.)*

JOHNNY. —Don't go.

JULIA. I wouldn't think of it.

JOHNNY. It'd be swell to have this whole day free with no ordeals to face.

JULIA. It'll be over soon.—I think we'll have Ned and Linda on our side.

JOHNNY. Lord, do they have to mix in, too?

JULIA. Well, they're my brother and sister.

JOHNNY. Are they good guys?

JULIA. —Dears. Ned's a little inclined to drink too much, but I think he'll outgrow it. You ought to be able to help him, I think. Linda's a curious girl. She's developed the queerest—I don't know—attitude toward life. I can't make her out. She doesn't think as we do at all, any more.

JOHNNY. We?

JULIA. —The family. Father's worried sick about her. I think *we* can help her a lot, though—I hope we can.

JOHNNY. *(Rises and goes to the fireplace)* She might prefer to work it out for herself. So might Ned.

JULIA. You *are* strange this morning, Johnny.

JOHNNY. How?

JULIA. You seem—not to like things quite as much as you might.

JOHNNY. Oh, yes, I do!

JULIA. We can't just wander forever up snowy mountains through pine woods with never a care, you know.

JOHNNY. Come here, darling. *(He goes to her, she to him. They meet.)* —We can do better than that.

JULIA. Do you suppose?

JOHNNY. I know. (JULIA's *head drops.*)

JULIA. Oh, I feel so awfully sad all at once.

JOHNNY. Don't—*don't.* Don't ever—— *(His grasp tightens upon her shoulders)* Look up here—! *(With an effort, she looks up.)* —Now please kiss me several times. *(She kisses him, once, twice, lightly.)*

JULIA. Is that all right?

JOHNNY. All right, hell. It's perfect. *(He bends to kiss her again, when the door suddenly opens and* LINDA SETON *enters, in hat and fur coat.* LINDA *is twenty-seven, and looks about twenty-two. She is slim, rather boyish, exceedingly fresh. She is smart, she is pretty, but beside* JULIA'S *grace,* JULIA'S *beauty, she seems a trifle gauche, and almost plain. She is pulling off her hat.)*

LINDA. I must say, that of all the boring—— *(She stops at the sight of* JULIA *and* JOHNNY*)* Why, Julia. For shame, Julia. (JULIA *and* JOHNNY *part.* LINDA *throws her hat and gloves upon a chair)* Is this a way to spend Sunday morning? Who's your partner? Anyone I know?

JULIA. It's—— *(She recovers her composure)* —This is Mr. Case—my sister, Linda.

JOHNNY. How do you do?

LINDA. Well, thanks.—And you?

JOHNNY. I couldn't be better.

LINDA. Good.

JULIA. *(With dignity)* —*Johnny* Case, his name is. I'm going to marry him.

LINDA. That makes it all right, then. *(She takes off her coat)* Who's coming to lunch? Susan and Nick didn't telephone, did they?

JULIA. —In just about one month I'm going to marry him.

LINDA. Stand over here in the light, will you, Case? (JOHNNY *turns to her scrutiny.)* —But I've never even seen you before.

JULIA. Neither had I, until ten days ago at Placid.

LINDA. *(To* JOHNNY, *with hope)* You aren't a guide, are you?

JOHNNY. No. I'm a lawyer.

LINDA. Wouldn't you know it.

JULIA. *(Seats herself upon a chair at Right)* I want you to be maid-of-honor, Linda.

LINDA. I accept. What'll we wear? *(She sits upon the bench at Left, and* JOHNNY *upon the sofa facing her.)* Listen: is this what came over Father in church?

JULIA. I imagine so.

LINDA. Then you've told him already.

JULIA. Yes.

LINDA. Tsch-tsch, this modern generation. *(To* JOHNNY*)* Well, young man, I hope you realize what you're getting in for.

(DELIA, *a housemaid of about thirty-five, comes in, takes* LINDA's *coat, hat and gloves, and goes out with them.)*

JULIA. That's pleasant.

LINDA. I don't mean you. You're divine. I mean Father—and Cousin Seton Cram and Laura and the rest of the outlying Setons—and the general atmosphere of plenty, with the top riveted down on the cornucopia——

JULIA. Johnny will try to bear up, won't you, Johnny?

JOHNNY. I'll do my best.

LINDA. *(Goes to* JULIA *and seats herself upon the bench facing her)* But how *did* you happen to get together? Tell Linda everything.

JULIA. Well, I was walking along the road with Miss Talcott one morning on the way to the rink and who should I see but——

LINDA. —*Whom* should I see but——

JULIA. —And who should I see but this man coming along, carrying skiis.

LINDA. Fancy that. A downright romance. Go on, dear——

JULIA. Do you really want to know?

LINDA. I'm hungry for romance, Sister. If you knew the way my little heart is beating against its bars right this minute.

JULIA. He had a queer look on his face.

LINDA. I can believe that. His eyes must have been burning.

JULIA. As a matter of fact, the trouble was with his nose. So I stopped him and said: "I suppose you don't realize it, but your nose is frozen." And he said: "Thanks, I hadn't realized it." And I said: "Well, it is." And he said: "I don't suppose there's anything you personally could do about it."

LINDA. Fresh.

JULIA. I thought so too.

JOHNNY. She was fresh to mention it. It looked to me like an out-and-out pick-up.

LINDA. Obviously.

JULIA. I know a good thing when I see it.

LINDA. *(To JOHNNY)* —So you swept her off her snowshoes?

JOHNNY. It was touch-and-go with us.

LINDA. *(To JULIA)* I think I like this man.

JULIA. I was sure you would.

LINDA. Well, my dears, take your happiness while you may.

JOHNNY. Watch us.

JULIA. *(Laughs)* No—*don't* watch us! Hello, Ned——

(NED SETON *enters from the hall. He is twenty-six. He is as handsome in his way as* JULIA *is in hers. His features are fine, a little too fine. He*

*displaces very little, but no one minds: he is a
nice boy.* JOHNNY *rises.* NED *goes to* JULIA.)

NED. Oh, *you're* back.—Then it was you who
took that shaker out of my room.

JULIA. This is Mr. Case—my brother Ned.
(JOHNNY *moves to* NED. *They shake hands briefly.)*

NED. How do you do?—It was you who took it,
Julia, and I'm getting sick of your meddling in my
affairs.

JULIA. I'm going to marry him. (NED *turns slowly,
as* JULIA's *words penetrate, and regards* JOHNNY.)

NED. You've got a familiar look about you.

JOHNNY. That's good.

NED. Is your name Johnny Case?

JOHNNY. Johnny Case.

NED. —One Saturday, quite a while ago, I went
down to New Haven for a game. Afterwards, you
took me all the way home from the Field, and put
me to bed somewhere.

LINDA. How sweet.

JOHNNY. Call me Nana. *(He goes to the sofa at
Right.)*

NED. I never got a chance to thank you. Thanks.

JOHNNY. It's all right.—Any time.

NED. *(Settles down with a newspaper on the sofa
at Left)* He's a good man, this Case fellow.

LINDA. The point is, there's no moss apparent, nor
yet the slightest touch of decay.

NED. I expect Father'll be a job. When do they
come to grips?

JULIA. Before luncheon, I suppose.

LINDA. *(Rises)* That soon? See here, Case, *I*
think you need some coaching.

JOHNNY. I'd be grateful for anything in this
trouble.

LINDA. Have you anything at all but your winning
way to your credit?

JOHNNY. Not a thing.

JULIA. Oh, hasn't he, though!

LINDA. The first thing Father will want to know is, how are you fixed?

JOHNNY. Fixed?

LINDA. *(Firmly)* —Fixed.—Are you a man of means, and if so, how much?

JULIA. Linda!

LINDA. Be still, Beauty. *(To* JOHNNY*)* I know you wouldn't expect that of a man in Father's position, but the fact is, money is our god here.

JULIA. Linda, I'll——! —Johnny, it isn't true at all.

NED. *(Looks up from his paper)* No?—What is, then?

LINDA. Well, young man?

JOHNNY. *(Goes to her)* I have in my pocket now, thirty-four dollars, and a package of Lucky Strikes. Will you have one?

LINDA. Thanks. *(She takes a cigarette from him)* —But no gilt-edged securities? No rolling woodlands?

JOHNNY. I've got a few shares of common stock tucked away in a warm place.

LINDA. —Common? Don't say the word. *(She accepts a light from him)* I'm afraid it won't do, Julia.—He's a comely boy, but probably just another of the vast army of clock-watchers. *(She moves toward the window.* JOHNNY *laughs and seats himself on the sofa at Right.)*

NED. *(From behind his newspaper)* How are you socially?

JOHNNY. Nothing there, either.

LINDA. *(Turning)* You mean to say your mother wasn't even a Whoozis?

JOHNNY. Not even that.

JULIA. Linda, I do wish you'd shut up.

NED. Maybe he's got a judge somewhere in the family.

LINDA. Yes, that might help. Old Judge Case's boy. White pillars. Guitars a-strummin'. Evenin', Massa.

NED. You must know some prominent people. Drop a few names.

LINDA. —Just casually, you know: "When I was to Mrs. Onderdonk's cock-fight last Tuesday, whom should I see but Mrs. Marble. Well, sir, I thought we'd die laughing——"

JULIA. *(To* JOHNNY*)* This is a lot of rot, you know.

JOHNNY. I'm having a grand time.

LINDA. " 'Johnny,' she says to me—she calls me 'Johnny'——"

JULIA. Oh, will you be *quiet!* What on earth has set you off this time?

LINDA. But it's dreadful, Sister. *(To* JOHNNY*)* —Just what do you think you're going to prove with Edward Seton, financier and cotillion-leader?

JOHNNY. Well, I'll tell you: when I find myself in a position like this, I ask myself: What would General Motors do? Then I do the opposite.

LINDA. *(Laughs and reseats herself. To* JULIA*)* It'll be a pity, if it doesn't come off. It'll be a real pity.

JULIA. It will come off. *(To* JOHNNY*)* Father isn't at all as they say he is.

JOHNNY. No?

JULIA. Not in the least.—Ned, where is he? Didn't he come in with you?

JOHNNY. Don't hurry him. There's no hurry.

NED. He said he had to stop to see Sam Hobson about something.

JULIA. *(To* JOHNNY*)* You.

JOHNNY. That's nice. I hope I get a good character.

LINDA. If it does go through all right, are you really going to make it quick?

JULIA. The second week in January. The tenth.

LINDA. —Announcing when?

JULIA. Right away—next Saturday, say.

LINDA. *(Eagerly)* Oh, darling, let me give a party for it!

JULIA. *(Puzzled)* Do you want to? I thought you hated the thought of——

LINDA. *I* want to! Not Father. *I* want to.

JULIA. Why, of course, dear. We'd love it.

NED. Who'd like a drink? *(No one bothers with him.)*

LINDA. —Father's to have nothing to do with it. And we *won't* send out cards. I'll telephone people. —Saturday's New Year's Eve, do you know it? Oh, Lord, Lord—let's have some fun in this house before you leave it!

JULIA. Why, Linda——

LINDA. I mean it! Let me, won't you?

JULIA. If Father doesn't mind.

LINDA. No ifs at all!—And just a few people— very few. Not a single bank of pink roses and no String Quartet during supper. All I want by way of entertainment is just one good tap-dancer. Let me plan it. Let me give it. Julia, let *me* do something for you once—*me*, Julia.

JULIA. I'd love it, dear. I really would.

LINDA. It won't be a ball, it'll be a simple sit-down supper—and you know where?—The old playroom.

JULIA. Why, not the——

LINDA. —Because the playroom's the one room in this house anyone's ever had fun in!

NED. I haven't been up there for ten years.

LINDA. That's your loss, Neddy. I've installed a new fangled gramophone, and I sit and play to myself by the hour. Come up some time. It's worth the trip. *(She turns suddenly to* JOHNNY*)* —Do you know any living people, Case? That's a cry from the heart.

JOHNNY. One or two.

LINDA. Give me a list. *(To* JULIA*)* —Seton and Laura can't have a look-in—is that understood? *(To* JOHNNY*)* —A terrible cousin and his wife—the Seton Crams. They're coming for lunch today. I hope your digestion's good. *(To* JULIA*)* —Not a look-in, remember.

JULIA. I don't know how you'll keep them out.

LINDA. *(Rises abruptly)* Oh, Julia—this is important to me!—No one must touch my party but me, do you hear?

JULIA. All right, darling.

LINDA. If anyone does, I won't come to it.

NED. —At that, you might have a better time. *(He rises)* Look here, Case——

JOHNNY. Yes?

NED. Cocktails aren't allowed at mid-day, so just before luncheon's announced I'll ask you if you care to brush up.

JOHNNY. And guess what I'll say.

JULIA. There'll be wine with lunch, Ned.

NED. You have to give it something to build on, don't you? *(A BUZZER sounds twice.* JULIA *and* JOHNNY *rise.)*

JULIA. —It's Father! He's home.

LINDA. He'll go up to his sitting-room first.

JULIA. *(Moves toward the door)* I know. Come on with me, Ned.

NED. I don't want to see him.

JULIA. Please come with me. *(*NED *goes out. She turns to* JOHNNY*)* You wait here with Linda a moment. I'll either come down again or send word. Just talk a while. *(She follows* NED *out. A brief pause. Then* LINDA *goes to the bench at Left, and* JOHNNY *to the one at Right.)*

LINDA. However do you do, Mr Case?

JOHNNY. —And you, Miss—uh——?

LINDA. Seton is the name.

JOHNNY. Not one of the bank Setons!

LINDA. The same.

JOHNNY. Fancy!—I hear a shipment of ear-marked gold is due in on Monday. *(Now they are seated.)*

LINDA. *(In her most social manner)* Have you been to the Opera much lately?

JOHNNY. Only in fits and starts, I'm afraid.

LINDA. But, my dear, we must do *something* for them! They entertained us in Rome.

JOHNNY. —And you *really* saw Mount Everest?

LINDA. Chit.

JOHNNY. Chat.

LINDA. Chit-chat.

JOHNNY. Chit-chat.

LINDA. Will that go for the preliminaries?

JOHNNY. It's all right with me.

LINDA. I love my sister Julia more than anything else in this world.

JOHNNY. I don't blame you. So do I.

LINDA. She's so sweet, you don't know.

JOHNNY. Yes, I do.

LINDA. She's beautiful.

JOHNNY. She's all of that.

LINDA. —And exciting, too—don't you think?

JOHNNY. —Don't. I'll start gittering.

LINDA. It's terribly important that she should marry the right person.

JOHNNY. That's important for everyone.

LINDA. It's particularly so for Julia.—I suppose you realize you're a rather strange bird in these parts.

JOHNNY. How's that?

LINDA. You don't know the kind of men we see as a rule.—Where have you been?

JOHNNY. Oh—working hard.

LINDA. Nights?

JOHNNY. Nights too.

LINDA. What about these little jaunts to Placid? Come clean, Case.

JOHNNY. That's the first holiday I've ever had.

LINDA. *(Unconvinced)* Yes.

JOHNNY. You heard what I said.

LINDA. Then you can't have been working long.

JOHNNY. Just since I was ten. *(She frowns, puzzled.)*

LINDA. —Ten. At what?

JOHNNY. —Anything I could get. Law, the last few years.

LINDA. —Must be ambitious.

JOHNNY. *(Expels his breath in a long, tired jet)* I am. Not for that, though.

LINDA. For what, then?

JOHNNY. Oh—to live. Do you mind? *(There is a pause.)*

LINDA. What is it you've been doing?

JOHNNY. I don't call what I've been doing, living.

LINDA. No? *(He shakes his head.)*

JOHNNY. —A while ago you asked me if I knew any living people. I know damn few.

LINDA. There aren't but damn few.

JOHNNY. Well, I mean to be one of them some day. Johnny's dream.

LINDA. So do I. Linda's longing.

JOHNNY. There's a pair called Nick and Susan Potter——

LINDA. So you know Nick and Susan?

JOHNNY. I should say I do.

LINDA. So that's where I've heard your name. Aren't they grand?

JOHNNY. It seems to me they know just about everything. Maybe I'm wrong.

LINDA. You're not, though.

JOHNNY. Life must be swell when you have some idea of what goes on, the way they do.

LINDA. They get more fun out of nothing than anyone I know.

JOHNNY. You don't have such a bad time yourself, do you?

LINDA. *(Leaning forward)* Case, are you drawing me out? (JOHNNY *laughs.)*

JOHNNY. Sure! Come on!

LINDA. Well, compared to the time I have, the last man in a chain-gang thoroughly enjoys himself.

JOHNNY. But how does that happen?

LINDA. You tell me, and I'll give you a rosy red apple.

JOHNNY. It seems to me you've got everything.

LINDA. Oh, it does, does it?

JOHNNY. What's the matter? Are you fed up?

LINDA. —To the neck.—Now tell me about *your* operation.

JOHNNY. I had been ailing for years—I don't know—life seemed to have lost its savor——

LINDA. Couldn't you do your housework?

JOHNNY. Every time I ran upstairs I got all rundown. (LINDA *laughs.* JOHNNY *leans forward)* You'd better come on a party with Julia and me.

LINDA. Any time you need an extra girl, give me a ring.—When?

JOHNNY. How's Tuesday?

LINDA. Splendid, thanks.—And how's Thursday?

JOHNNY. Blooming.

LINDA. *(Reflectively)* —Looked badly the last time we met.

JOHNNY. —Just nerves, nothing but nerves.

LINDA. *(A moment's pause. Then)* —Do I seem to you to complain a good deal?

JOHNNY. I hadn't noticed it.

LINDA. Then I can let myself go a little: this is a hell of a life, Case.

JOHNNY. *(Looks about him)* What do you mean? All this luxe? All this——?

LINDA. You took the words right out of my mouth.

JOHNNY. Well, for that matter, so's mine.

LINDA. What's the answer?

JOHNNY. Maybe you need some time off, too—I mean from what you're doing, day in, day out——

LINDA. *Days* out, please—*years* out——

JOHNNY. All right: take it. Take the time——

LINDA. —And of course *that's* so easy.

JOHNNY. —It can be done. *I* intend to do it. I intend to take quite a lot of it—when I'm not so busy just making the wherewithal.

LINDA. Case, you astonish me. I thought you were a Willing Worker.

JOHNNY. I am, if I can get what I'm working for.

LINDA. And what would that be?

JOHNNY. Mine is a simple story: I just want to save part of my life for myself. There's a catch to it, though. It's got to be part of the young part.

LINDA. You'll never get on and up that way.

JOHNNY. All right, but I want *my* time while I'm young. And let me tell you, the minute I get hold of just about twenty nice round thousands, I'm going to knock off for as long as they last, and——

LINDA. Quit?

JOHNNY. Quit. Retire young, and work old. That's what I want to do.

LINDA. —Grand. Does Julia know about it?

JOHNNY. No—there's no use getting her hopes up until it happens.—Don't tell her, will you?

LINDA. She has enough of her own for two right now—or ten, for that matter. Mother and Grandfather did us pretty pretty.

JOHNNY. *(Shakes his head)* Thanks, but I've got to do myself—only just pretty enough.

LINDA. I see. That's foolish—but you're all right, Case. You haven't been bitten with it yet—you haven't been caught by it.

JOHNNY. By what?

LINDA. *(So reverently)* The reverence for riches.

JOHNNY. *(Laughs)* You *are* a funny girl.

LINDA. —Funny, am I? And what about you, you big stiff?

JOHNNY. *(Laughs, and rises)* —Just take Johnny's hand, and come into the Light, sister. (JULIA *enters.* JOHNNY *turns to her)* Did you see him?

JULIA. I saw him.

LINDA. Julia! How was he?

JULIA. I don't know yet.—Johnny, you go up to Ned's room. You haven't arrived yet. Take the elevator—Father's coming down the stairs. Quick, will you?

JOHNNY. When do I arrive?

JULIA. One o'clock. It's quarter to.

JOHNNY. This is getting a little complicated, if you ask me.

JULIA. Nobody asked you. Go on! Do as you're told.

JOHNNY. *(Turns)* See here, you saucy——

LINDA. *(Goes to the fireplace)* Go on, Case. Don't expect simplicity here—just think of our Fifth Avenue frontage. (JOHNNY *laughs and goes out.* LINDA *turns to* JULIA) Tell me: was Father awful?

JULIA. —The same old story, of course: I'm being married for my money.

LINDA. That's always flattering.—But Case didn't know our foul secret, did he?

JULIA. No.

LINDA. Even if he had, what of it?—And what good's all this jack we've got, anyway—unless to get us a superior type of husband?

JULIA. I hate you to talk like that! I hate it!

LINDA. Listen to me, Julia: I'm sore all the way

through. I've been sore for a long time now, ever
since I really saw how it—oh, never mind. Anyway,
I don't doubt that if Case *had* known he'd still be
running. You're in luck there.

JULIA. You do like him, don't you?

LINDA. She asks me if I like him!—My dear girl,
do you realize that *life* walked into this house this
morning? Marry him quick. Don't let him get away.
And if Father starts the usual—where *is* Big Business, anyhow?

JULIA. He said he'd be right down.

LINDA. Stand your ground, Julia. If you don't
know your own mind by now, you haven't got a
mind. Name your date and stick to it. I'm telling
you.

JULIA. *(Slowly)* I want Father to see that Johnny
has the selfsame qualities Grandfather had,—and
that there's no reason why he shouldn't arrive just
where he did.

LINDA. —If he wants to.

JULIA. —Wants to! You don't know Johnny.
You don't know how far he's come already—and
from what——

LINDA. —Or where he's going.

JULIA. *I* do! *I* know! I can see it clear as day!
(A moment. Then) Linda——

LINDA. What?

JULIA. It'll be awful to leave you.

LINDA. I don't know exactly what I'll do, when
you go. I've got to do something—get out—quit on
it—change somehow, or I'll go mad. I could curl up
and die right now.

JULIA. *(Touched)* Why, darling——

LINDA. Why, my foot. I don't look sick, do I?
(She moves to the fireplace) Oh, Lord, if I could
only get *warm* in this barn! *(She crouches before
the fire and holds her hands to it)* —Never mind
about me. I'll be all right. Look out for yourself.

When Big Business comes down, just watch you don't let him—— *(The door opens. She looks over her shoulder and sees her Father)* —But by a strange coincidence, here he is now.

JULIA. Did you see Mr. Hobson, Father?

(EDWARD SETON enters. He is fifty-eight, large, nervous, distinguished. He wears a black morning coat, a white carnation in the buttonhole, and gray striped trousers. He takes nose glasses from his nose and folds them away in a silver case.)

EDWARD. Yes.—Of course, my dear, there is another thing to be considered: What is the young man's background? Is he the sort of person that—? Ah, good morning, Linda.

LINDA. You saw me in church, Father. What's on your mind? You look worried.

EDWARD. I presume Julia has told you her story?

LINDA. Story? She's told me the facts.

EDWARD. But we mustn't rush into things, must we? *(A glance passes between JULIA and LINDA.)*

JULIA. *(Goes to him)* I want to be married on January tenth, Father. That's—that's just two weeks from Tuesday.

EDWARD. *(Moves to the table behind the sofa at Right, and begins to search through the newspapers)* Quite impossible.

LINDA. Why?

JULIA. Yes, why? I—I'm sure I couldn't stand a long engagement.

EDWARD. As yet, there is no engagement to stand.

LINDA. The boy has loads of charm, Father.

EDWARD. *(Quickly)* You know him?

LINDA. I've heard tell of him.

EDWARD. *(Tastes the word)* Charm.

LINDA. —I suppose it's solid merit you're after.

Well, the rumor is he's got that, too. Sterling chap, on the whole. A catch, in fact. (NED *wanders in and seats himself upon the sofa at Left, with a newspaper.*)

JULIA. What did Mr. Hobson say, Father?

EDWARD. We must find out about the young man's background.

JULIA. What did he say?

EDWARD. Have you the financial section of the *Times,* Ned?

NED. No, I try to take Sundays off, when I can.

EDWARD. —Which reminds me: I should like you to make a practice of remaining in the office until six o'clock.

NED. Six!—What for?

EDWARD. As an example to the other men.

NED. But there's nothing for me to do after three.

EDWARD. You will find something.

NED. Look here, Father—if you think I'm going to fake a lot of——

EDWARD. Did you understand me, Ned? *(A moment:* NED *loses.)*

NED. —Oh, all right.

JULIA. What did Mr. Hobson say about Johnny, Father?

EDWARD. *(Settles himself upon the sofa with the financial section, now happily found)* His report was not at all unfavorable.

LINDA. That must have been a blow.

JULIA. —But what did he *say?*

EDWARD. We must find out more about the young man, Julia. He seems to have some business ability —he has put through what looks like a successful reorganization of Seaboard Utilities. He holds some of the stock.

NED. Seaboard! Poor fellow——

EDWARD. —Shrewd fellow, perhaps. Hobson says

signs are not unfavorable for Seaboard.—We'll buy some in the morning, Ned.

LINDA. Just another ill wind blowing money to Da-Da.

EDWARD. But we *must* know more about Mr. Chase's background.

JULIA. Case, Father, Case.

LINDA. Let it go. Chase has such a sweet banking sound.

JULIA. He's from Baltimore.

LINDA. Fine old pre-war stock, I imagine.

NED. Wasn't there a Judge Case somewhere?

EDWARD. We shall see. We shall take steps to—

LINDA. Father, if you reach for a Social Register, I'll cry out with pain.

EDWARD. *(With decision)* Well, I most certainly intend to know more about the young man than his name and his birthplace.—He does not, of course, realize that you have spoken to me, as yet?

NED. Of course not.

LINDA. Julia works fast, but not *that* fast, do you, Julia? (JULIA *does not answer.)*

EDWARD. I propose not to allow the subject of an engagement to come up in my first talk with him. I believe I am competent to direct the conversation.— You and Ned, Julia, may excuse yourselves on one pretext or another. I should like you to stay, Linda.

LINDA. I *knew* I should have learned shorthand. (EDWARD *smiles.* HENRY *enters.)*

EDWARD. I shall trust your memory.—Yes, Henry?

HENRY. Mr. Case wishes to be announced, sir.

EDWARD. Yes. (HENRY *goes out, closing the door after him.* EDWARD *arranges his cuffs, and takes a firmer seat in his chair.)*

LINDA. —So does Mr. Case's engagement. I want to give a party for it New Year's Eve, Father.

JULIA. Wait a minute, dear——

EDWARD. *(Watching the doorway)* You may give

a party if you like, Linda, but whether to announce an engagement, we shall see——

LINDA. —Another point about my party is that it's *my* party—mine.

EDWARD. Yes?

LINDA. Yes—and as such, I'd like to run it. I can do quite well without your secretary this time, darling—and without Seton's and Laura's helpful hints, I can do brilliantly.—There's someone at the door.

NED. Keep a stiff upper lip, Father. No doubt the fellow is an impostor.

EDWARD. *(Laughs)* Oh, we shall learn many things this morning! He is not the first young man to be interviewed by me.

JULIA. Father——

EDWARD. Yes, daughter?

JULIA. Remember: I know what I want. (JOHNNY *enters.)* Oh, here you are!

JOHNNY. Here I am.

JULIA. Father, this is—Mr. Case. (JOHNNY *goes to* EDWARD. *They shake hands.* NED *rises.)*

EDWARD. How do you do, Mr. Case?

JOHNNY. How do you do, sir?

EDWARD. —My daughter, Linda.

LINDA. How do you do?

JOHNNY. How do you do?

EDWARD. And my son, Ned.

JOHNNY. How do you do?

NED. I recall your face, but your figure puzzles me.

EDWARD. Julia, if you and Ned will do the telephoning I spoke of, Linda and I will try to entertain Mr. Case until the others come—won't we, Linda?

LINDA. Sure. I'm game.

JULIA. *(Moves toward the door)* —Coming, Ned?

NED. *(Following her)* I wonder what we'd do without the telephone. *(They go out.)*

EDWARD. Sit down, Mr. Case.

JOHNNY. Thank you. *(He seats himself upon the bench, Left, and* LINDA *upon a small stool at the fireplace.)*

EDWARD. I presume, like all young people, you have the bad habit of smoking before luncheon?

JOHNNY. I'm afraid I have.

EDWARD. —A cigar?

JOHNNY. Not right now, thank you.

EDWARD. *(Lets himself down into a sofa)* We've been quite at the mercy of the snow these days, haven't we?

JOHNNY. It doesn't seem much after Placid.

EDWARD. Placid—ah, yes! My daughter Julia has just come from there.

JOHNNY. I know.

EDWARD. *(A brief pause. Then)* —You are in business in New York, Mr. Case?

JOHNNY. Yes, I'm in the Law. I'm with Sloan, Hobson.

EDWARD. An excellent firm.—And a born New Yorker?

JOHNNY. No. I was born in Baltimore.—In eighteen ninety-seven. July sixth. I'm thirty.

EDWARD. Baltimore—I used to have many friends in Baltimore.—The Whites—the Clarence Whites— Possibly you knew them.

JOHNNY. No, I don't believe I ever did.

EDWARD. —And then there was Archie Fuller's family——

JOHNNY. I'm afraid not.

EDWARD. —And let me see now—Colonel Evans —old Philip Evans——

JOHNNY. Nope. *(There is a silence. Then)* I haven't been there in some years. And I shouldn't be likely to know them, anyway. My mother and father died when I was quite young. My father had a small grocery store in Baltimore, which he was never able to make a go of. He left a number of debts which my mother worked very hard to clear up. I was the only child, and I wasn't in a position to help very much. She died the May before my sixteenth birthday. (LINDA *is listening with growing interest.*)

EDWARD. But how sad.

JOHNNY. It *was* pretty sad.—I hadn't any connections, except for an uncle who's in the roofing business in Wilmington. He wasn't much good, though—he was inclined to get drunk—still is——

LINDA. We have an uncle like that, but he keeps off roofs.

JOHNNY. *(Smiles at her, and continues)* —But I was what's called a bright boy, and I managed to wangle a couple of scholarships. They helped a good deal in school and college, and there were always plenty of ways to make up the difference. In term-time I usually ran eating-joints and typed lecture notes. In summers I sold aluminum pots and pans——

EDWARD. *(Weakly)* Linda! Are you there, Linda?

LINDA. Yes, Father.

JOHNNY. —Or worked in a factory or on a newspaper. Once I got myself engaged as a tutor. That was pretty unpleasant. Then there were department stores at Christmas and florists at Easter. During law school I slept all night on a couch in a doctor's office, and got fifteen a week for it. That was soft.

EDWARD. *(It is all he can say)* Admirable!

JOHNNY. No—it simply happened to be the only way to get through. *(A brief pause. Then)* Anything else, sir?

EDWARD. I beg your pardon?

LINDA. *(Rises)* I should think you would.

JOHNNY. —Is there anything more I can tell you about myself?

EDWARD. Why, uh—that is to say, uh—— *(He flounders and stops. A moment, then* JOHNNY *moves toward him.)*

JOHNNY. Well, Mr. Seton, how about it?

EDWARD. About it? About what?

JOHNNY. Julia and me.

EDWARD. You and Julia? I'm afraid I——

JOHNNY. —About our getting married.

EDWARD. *(There is a silence. Then)* This is a complete surprise, Mr. Case. I don't know quite what to say to you.

JOHNNY. *(Smiles)* "Yes" would be pleasant.

EDWARD. I am sure it would. However, we must go into it rather more carefully, I am afraid.

JOHNNY. The only difficulty is the time. Julia's idea is January tenth. It's mine, too.

EDWARD. We shall see about that.

JOHNNY. May I ask *how* we shall see, sir?

EDWARD. Mr. Case, I do not know you at all.

JOHNNY. I'll give you every opportunity you permit me. How's lunch tomorrow?

EDWARD. Tomorrow I have several——

JOHNNY. —Tuesday?

EDWARD. *(Hesitates)* Will you meet me at the Bankers' Club at one on Friday?

JOHNNY. I'm terribly sorry, but Friday's out. I've got to go to Boston on business.—Better make it tomorrow. *(A moment.* NED *and* JULIA *re-enter. Then* EDWARD *speaks, hastily:)*

EDWARD. —Very well. I shall arrange my appointments.—Ah, Ned, Julia—and what do you suppose can be keeping the Crams? *(But* JOHNNY *cuts in before they can reply:)*

JOHNNY. —Thank you. In the meantime, I think Mr. Hobson or Mr. Sloan might say a good word for me. I'm nobody at all, as things go. But I'm quite decent and fairly civilized, and I love your daughter very much—which isn't a bit hard. She seems to like me quite a lot too, and that's about all that can be said for me—except that I think we've a simply grand chance to be awfully happy.—What do *you* say, Julia?

JULIA. Oh, so do I!

LINDA. Come on, Father, be an angel. *I* think he's a very good number.

EDWARD. I am afraid it is too important a matter to be decided off-hand.

JULIA. But I want to be married on the——

EDWARD. *(With sudden sharpness)* You will be married, Julia, when I have reached a favorable decision—and upon a day which I will name.

JULIA. I—our plan was—the tenth, and sail that night on——

EDWARD. The tenth is out of the question.

JULIA. Oh, but Father——! I——

EDWARD. —And we shall let it rest at that, for the moment.

LINDA. But you'll come round, Father! I have a swell hunch you'll come round. Oh, Lordy, Lordy, what fun! Let's all join hands and—— *(VOICES are heard from the hall.)*

EDWARD. Seton?—Laura?—Is that you I hear?

LINDA. You bet it is.—Let's *not* join hands.

(SETON CRAM and his wife, LAURA, enter. SETON is thirty-six, somewhat bald, inclined to a waist-line, but well turned out in a morning coat, striped trousers and spats. LAURA is thirty-two, a shade taller than SETON, with a rather handsome, rather disagreeable face. She is as smartly dressed as a poor figure will allow.)

SETON. Hello, hello!

EDWARD. —How are you, young man?

SETON. Blooming, thanks. We walked all the way up. *(They shake hands with* EDWARD.*)*

LAURA. I do hope we're not late, Uncle Ned.

EDWARD. No, indeed!

LINDA. You're early.

LAURA. Julia, my dear, you're back. *(She kisses her and then bears down upon* LINDA*)* —And Linda! How simply stunning!

LINDA. *(Wards off the impending kiss)* Careful, Laura—I've got the most terrible cold.

LAURA. *(Returning)* But I never saw you looking better!—Hello, Ned.

NED. Hello. *(Warn CURTAIN.)*

EDWARD. This is—uh—Mr. Case—my nephew, Mr. Cram, and Mrs. Cram. (LAURA *inclines her head.)*

SETON. How do you do?

JOHNNY. How do you do? (NED *edges away from* LAURA. EDWARD, *still stunned, stares in front of himself.)*

LAURA. —Isn't it horrid how chapped one's hands get this weather? I don't know *what* to do. How was Placid, Julia?—You must have had *such* a divine time. Were there loads of amusing people there?—And lots of beaux, too—— Oh, you needn't deny it!—We know Julia, don't we, Seton?—And you, Linda—we haven't seen *you* for ages—— *(She seats herself upon the bench at Right)* —Now sit right down and tell us *everything* you've been doing——

LINDA. Well, take the average day: I get up about eight-thirty, bathe, dress, and have my coffee. —Aren't you going to brush up before lunch, Ned?

NED. —Would you care to brush up before lunch, Case?

JOHNNY. I think I shall, if I may. *(He follows* NED *to the door.)*

LINDA. —Julia?

JULIA. I'm all right, thanks.

LINDA. But look at *me*, will you! *(She moves quickly across the room after* NED *and* JOHNNY, *flecking imaginary dust from her dress as she goes)* —Simply *covered* with dust!—Wait, boys!

CURTAIN

ACT TWO

SCENE: *The Playroom on the top floor is a long and spacious low-ceilinged room with white woodwork and pale blue walls upon which are lightly traced story-book designs in silver, white and green.*

At Right and Left there are two windows with window seats below them, curtained in a white-starred cretonne of a deeper blue than the walls.

The only entrance is from the hall at Back.

At Right there is a low platform for horizontal bars and a punching-bag, above which a pair of trapezes swing from the ceiling. At present they are tied up. Against the back wall behind them is a glass cabinet containing a collection of old toys, arranged on shelves in orderly rows.

Also at Right is a table, with tablecloth spread, and four small chairs. Against the back wall at Left is an old-fashioned music-box, and in the corner near it a small electric gramophone. Also at Left is a low couch and a table, a miniature easy-chair and a folding cushion.

TIME: *New Year's Eve, this year.*

AT RISE: *The Playroom is empty, and lit only by a pale NIGHT GLOW from the windows. A moment, then* JULIA *opens the door, and calls:*

40

JULIA. Linda! *(There is no answer. Dance MUSIC is heard from downstairs.)* She isn't here.

NED. *(Reaches past her to an electric button and lights the room)* I didn't say she was. All I said was it's where she comes, as a rule, when she finds herself in a jam. *(They come into the room. BOTH are in evening clothes. In one hand NED carries two whisky and sodas. He puts one glass on the table and retains the other.)*

JULIA. I don't believe she's in the house.

NED. *(Takes a swallow of his drink)* Maybe not.

JULIA. I told them all at dinner that she had a blinding headache, but expected to come down later.

NED. That's as good as anything—— *(And another swallow)* Let's get out of here. This room gives me a funny feeling.

JULIA. Wait a minute.—You know how furious Father was when she wasn't there for dinner—— *(She goes and shuts the door, closing out the MUSIC)* What can we do, Ned?

NED. Search me.

JULIA. *(She moves to a chair and seats herself)* But it's her party!

NED. Don't make me laugh, Julia. It was, maybe, until you and Father took it over.

JULIA. *I* did?

NED. You stood by and saw it done. Then the Crams got hold of it. Among you, you asked the whole list—which was just what Linda didn't want. You threw out the team of dancers she'd engaged for supper, and got in that troupe of Scotch Songbirds. You let Farley, with his Flower Fancies, turn it into a house of mourning. Among you, you made Linda's funny little bust into a first-class funeral. I can't say I blame her, no. However—*(He raises his glass)* —drink to Linda.

JULIA. Well, I do! She should have realized that

Father couldn't announce my engagement without *some* fuss.

NED. She should have, yes. But unlike me, Linda always hopes. *(Again his glass is raised)* Bottoms up to Linda.

JULIA. Don't, Ned.

NED. Don't what?

JULIA. You've been drinking steadily since eight o'clock.

NED. Yes?—Funny old Ned. On New Year's Eve, too. *(He drains his glass and takes up the other.)*

JULIA. Will you kindly stop it?

NED. Darling sister, I shall drink as much as I like at any party I agree to attend. *(She turns from him with an exclamation.)* —And as much as I like is as much as I can hold. It's my protection against your tiresome friends. Linda's out of luck, she hasn't one.

JOHNNY. *(Comes in. MUSIC and VOICES are heard from downstairs)* —Believe it or not, I've been talking politics with an Admiral. *(He looks about him)* —What a nice room!

NED. It's too full of ghosts for me. It gives me the creeps.

JULIA. She isn't here, Johnny.

JOHNNY. Linda?

JULIA. Yes, of course.

JOHNNY. Did you expect she would be?

JULIA. Ned thought so.

NED. Ned was wrong.

(HENRY *and* CHARLES *enter.* HENRY *carries table linen and silver and a tray of plates and glasses;* CHARLES *a pail of ice containing two bottles of champagne and a plate of sandwiches. They go to the table.)*

JULIA. Isn't there room for everyone downstairs, Henry?

HENRY. Miss Linda telephoned to serve supper here for six at half-past eleven, Miss.

NED. Ned was right.

JULIA. From where did she telephone, do you know?

HENRY. She didn't say, Miss. *(There is a pause.* HENRY *and* CHARLES *proceed to set the table.)*

JOHNNY. *(To* JULIA*)* I think I know where she is, if that's any help.

JULIA. You? Where—?

JOHNNY. With Nick and Susan Potter.

JULIA. What's she doing with them?

JOHNNY. Dining, I imagine.

NED. It's eleven-twenty now.

JULIA. Where did you get your information, Johnny?

JOHNNY. I met her coming in this afternoon. She said she wouldn't stay in the house tonight. Apparently it meant more to her than anyone thought.

NED. Not than I thought. I warned Father.

JOHNNY. It was no use talking to her. She was going out to dine somewhere by herself. I knew that Nick and Susan were having Pete Jessup and Mary Hedges, so I telephoned Susan and asked her to ask Linda, too.

JULIA. I wish you had spoken to me first.

JOHNNY. Why?

JULIA. People like that aren't good for Linda.

JOHNNY. *(Looks at her for a moment, puzzled, and then laughs)* What are you talking about, Julia?

JULIA. They make her even more discontented than she is. Heavens knows why, but they do.

NED. Apparently she's bringing them back with her. (HENRY *and* CHARLES *go out, closing the door after them.)*

JULIA. Well, they certainly can't expect to have supper up here by themselves.

NED. No? Why not?

JULIA. They simply can't, that's all.

NED. What is this conspiracy against Linda, anyway? Are you all afraid she might cause a good time here, for once—and if she did, the walls might fall down? Is that it? (JULIA *does not reply.* JOHNNY *seats himself near her.*)

JOHNNY. I do love this room, don't you, Julia?

JULIA. *(Briefly)* Yes.—It was Mother's idea for us.

JOHNNY. She must have been sweet.

JULIA. She was.

NED. —Father wanted a big family, you know. So she had Julia straight off, to oblige him. But Julia was a girl, so she promptly had Linda. But Linda was a girl—it looked hopeless. *(His voice rises)* —So the next year she had me, and there was much joy in the land.—It was a boy, and the fair name of Seton would flourish. (JULIA *looks at him in alarm.*) —It must have been a great consolation to Father. Drink to Mother, Johnny—she tried to be a Seton for a while, then gave up and died.—Drink to Mother——

JOHNNY. *(Laughs uneasily)* You're talking through your hat, Ned.

NED. But I'm not.

JULIA. *(To* JOHNNY*)* Can't you possibly persuade him that he's had enough?

NED. It's all right, Julia: you heard what I said. —There's a bar in my room, if you want anything, Johnny. Tell as many of the men as you think need it. It's all very pleasant and hole-in-the-wall like everything else that's any relief in this house.— Drink to Father. *(He drains his glass, sets it down upon a table, turns on his heel and goes out, closing the door after him.)*

JULIA. We must do something about them—we *must,* Johnny!

JOHNNY. —Him and Linda.

JULIA. Yes, yes!

JOHNNY. I don't see what.—It seems a lot more goes on inside them than we've any idea of. Linda must be at the end of some rope or other. As for Ned——

JULIA. He always does this—always——

JOHNNY. *(Rises)* He began some time.—I'll keep an eye on him, though, and if he stops making sense I'll get him to bed somehow.

JULIA. —And Linda's got to bring her friends downstairs.—People know there's something wrong, now—they must know.—She's simply *got* to!

JOHNNY. All right, darling. Only——

JULIA. Only what——

JOHNNY. —Do try to enjoy tonight, won't you?

JULIA. But I am, Johnny. I think it's a lovely party!

JOHNNY. Then how about getting that frown from between your eyes and not feeling personally responsible for three hundred guests, and a brother and sister?

JULIA. —Someone's got to be.

JOHNNY. —Let your Father, then.

JULIA. Poor man. Reporters have been after him all day long.

JOHNNY. Me, too. I've never felt so important.

JULIA. I hope you didn't talk.

JOHNNY. I just asked for offers for the story of how I wooed and won you. Farm Boy Weds Heiress as Blizzard Grips City.

JULIA. *(Laughs)* What *did* you say?

JOHNNY. I didn't see them.

JULIA. That's right. Father was awfully anxious that nothing be added to what he sent in—except, of course, what they're bound to add themselves.

JOHNNY. Evidently it's a good deal.

JULIA. Well, that we can't help.

JOHNNY. The French Line wrote me. They want to give us a suite, in place of the cabin.

JULIA. I doubt if we ought to accept it.

JOHNNY. No? Why not?

JULIA. I think it might not look so well. I'll ask Father.

JOHNNY. *(A brief pause. Then)* Perhaps we oughtn't to go abroad at all. Perhaps *that's* too great an evidence of wealth.

JULIA. Now, Johnny——

JOHNNY. —But we're going, my dear, and in the most comfortable quarters they choose to provide.

JULIA. What a curious tone for you to take. *(He looks at her in amazement, then laughs genuinely.)*

JOHNNY. Julia, don't be ridiculous! "Tone to take." *(She turns from him.)* —We may be suddenly and unexpectedly important to the world, but I don't see that we're quite important enough to bend over backwards.

JULIA. *(A silence. Then)* Of course, I'll do whatever you like about it.

JOHNNY. It would be nice if you'd like it too.

JULIA. *(She returns to him)* And I'll like it too, Johnny. *(He bends and kisses her lightly.)*

JOHNNY. —Sweet. *(He takes her by the hand and draws her toward the door)* —Come on, let's go below and break into a gavotte.

JULIA. *(Stops)* —Do something for me, will you?

JOHNNY. Sure.

JULIA. —Stay here till Linda arrives, then make her come down. I can't wait. *Some* female member of the household's got to be around, if it's only the cook.

JOHNNY. —I'll *ask* her to come down.

JULIA. Insist on it!

JOHNNY. Well, I'll do whatever a gent can in the circumstances.

JULIA. You're *so* irritating! Honestly, I hate the sight of you.

JOHNNY. Julia——

JULIA. What?

JOHNNY. Like hell you do.

JULIA. I know. It's hopeless. *(She goes to the door, opens it, then turns to him again. LAUGH-TER is heard from downstairs.)* Do as you like—I love you very much.

JOHNNY. —You get through that door quick and close it after you, or you won't get out at all.

JULIA. —Just to look at you makes my spine feel like—feel like—— *(He moves swiftly toward her, but finds the door closed. He stands for a moment staring at it, transfixed, then pulls it open, calling "Darling!"—But instead of JULIA, he finds NICK POTTER.)*

NICK. Hey! What is this?

JOHNNY. Nick! *(NICK moves away from him, scowling, and straightening his coat. He is about thirty-four, with an attractive, amusing face.)*

NICK. —Get fresh with me, and I'll knock your block off. *(He sees the champagne and goes to it)* What have we here—some kind of a grape beverage?

JOHNNY. Mumm's the word.—Where's Susan?

NICK. Coming.—I hear you're engaged. Many happy returns. Is it announced yet?

JOHNNY. Thanks.—No, it's to come with a roll of drums at midnight—"A lady has lost a diamond and platinum wrist watch."

NICK. —With that gifted entertainer, Mr. Edward Seton, at the microphone——

JOHNNY. That's the plan.

NICK. I heard about his work with this party.—He has the true ashman's touch, that man.

JOHNNY. He's been all right to me.

NICK. Oh, sure—he believes you're a comer. That's what won him over so quickly—the same stuff as Grandpa Seton himself—up-from-nothing —hew to the line—eat yeast. Me—of course I'm God's great social menace because I never got out and did Big Things.

JOHNNY. I really like him. I like him a lot.

NICK. Keep your men on him, though. Don't relax your vigilance. *(He is opening the bottles and filling the glasses. MUSIC and VOICES are heard through the open door.)*

JOHNNY. —You think, for instance, that if *I* should quit business——

NICK. Just try it once. Why, he'd come down on you like Grant took Bourbon.

JOHNNY. You've got him all wrong, Nick.

NICK. Maybe.—Anyhow, you're not really thinking of it, are you?

JOHNNY. *(Goes to the couch)* I am, you know!

NICK. On what, may I ask?

JOHNNY. Well, I've got a nice little mess of common stock that's begun to move about two years before I thought it would. And if it goes where I think it will——

NICK. —Haven't you and Julia a pretty good life ahead as it is, Johnny?

JOHNNY. You and Susan have a better one.

NICK. Listen, baby—I don't think I'd try any enlightened living stuff on this family. They wouldn't know what you were talking about.

JOHNNY. Julia would.

NICK. —Might. But the old man's a terror, Johnny. Honestly—you don't *know.*

JOHNNY. Enough of your jibes, Potter. You answer to me for your slurs on a Seton.

NICK. *(Moves toward him)* —Seats on a Slurton —I want to get three seats on a Slurton for Tuesday night. *(—And confronts him with an empty bottle)* Go on, hit me, why don't you? Just hit me. Take off your glasses—*(And returns to the table)* —I was dragged against my will to this function. And somehow I don't seem to so well.

JOHNNY. What?

NICK. —Function.

*(*LINDA *and* SUSAN *enter.* SUSAN *is thirty, smart and attractive. She goes straight to* JOHNNY *and kisses him.)*

SUSAN. Cheers from me, Johnny.

JOHNNY. Thanks, Susan.

SUSAN *and* NICK. *(Together)* We only hope that you will be as happy as we have been. (LINDA *closes the door. VOICES and MUSIC cease to be heard.* NICK *continues to fill the glasses.)*

JOHNNY. *(To* LINDA*)* What did you do with Pete and Mary?

LINDA. They're coming in a heated barouche.

JOHNNY. Linda, I'm to inform you that there's another party going on in the house.

LINDA. You mean that low-class dance hall downstairs? *(She moves toward* NICK*)* Don't speak of it. (NICK *gives her a glass of wine, and then one to* SUSAN.*)*

NICK. Here, Pearl, wet your pretty whistle with this. (NICK *and* JOHNNY *take glasses.* SUSAN *raises hers.)*

SUSAN. —To Johnny and his Julia.

JOHNNY. Julia—— *(They drink.* LINDA *seats herself in a chair near the table.)*

SUSAN. —Merry Christmas, from Dan to Beersheba.

NICK. *(Examining the table)* —Only sandwiches? What a house!

LINDA. There's solid food on the way.

NICK. I'll trade twenty marbles and a jack-knife for the carcass of one chicken, in good repair.

LINDA. You should have been with us, Johnny. Not one word of sense was spoken from eight to eleven.

SUSAN. —When Linda got homesick.

LINDA. I'm a die-hard about this evening and this room. I only hope nobody else wanders in. (JOHNNY *seats himself near* LINDA.)

NICK. I tell you who'd be fun.

LINDA. Who?

NICK. Seton and Laura.

LINDA. They wouldn't stay long.—You see those trapezes?

NICK. Yes?

LINDA. Time was when Seton and I used to swing from them by our knees, and spit at each other.

NICK. Great!

LINDA. I'm happy to say now, I rarely missed.

JOHNNY. But aren't we going downstairs?

LINDA. No, Angel, we're not.

NICK. It's grand here. It takes sixty years off these old shoulders. *(He looks at his watch)* Eleven-forty.—Doctor Stork's on the way, dears, with Little Baby New Year. *(He goes and seats himself with* JOHNNY *and* LINDA.)

LINDA. I wish someone would tell me what *I'm* to do next year—and the year after—and the year after that——

SUSAN. What you need is a husband, Linda. *(She joins the group.)*

LINDA. Have you got any addresses?

SUSAN. He'll arrive. I only hope you'll know how to act when he does.

LINDA. Well, I won't take No for an answer.

NICK. Don't you do it.

LINDA. And in the meanwhile—what? Hot-foot it

around the world with a maid and a dog? Lie on one beach after another, getting brown?

NICK. Oo, I *love* to play in the sand.

SUSAN. *(To* LINDA*)* —You just won't stay put, will you, child?

LINDA. And grow up to be a committee-woman and sit on Boards? Excuse me, Susan, but from now on any charity work *I* do will be for the rich. They need it more. (NICK, SUSAN *and* JOHNNY *are eating sandwiches and sipping their wine.)*

NICK. Now look, Linda—let me tell you about yourself, will you?

LINDA. Go ahead.

NICK. There's more of your grandfather in you than you think.

LINDA. Boo.

NICK. There is, though. He wasn't satisfied with the life he was born into, so he made one for himself. Now, you don't like *his* five-story log cabin so you're out in the woods again with your own little hatchet.

SUSAN. The Little Pioneer, with Linda Seton.

JOHNNY. —Linda's off on the wrong foot, though. She's headed up the fun-alley. She thinks having fun is the whole answer to life.

LINDA. *I* do?

JOHNNY. You do.—Me—it's not just entertainment *I'm* after—oh, no—I want all of it—inside, outside—smooth and rough—let 'er come!

NICK. You're right, too.—Life's a grand little ride, if you take it yourself.

JOHNNY. —And no good at all if someone else takes you on it. Damn it, there's *no* life any good but the one you make for yourself.

SUSAN. *(A protest)* Hey, hey——

JOHNNY. —Except yours and Nick's, maybe.

LINDA. But they *have* made theirs!—Haven't you Susan?

Susan. About half-and-half, I should say. I don't know quite what we'd do if we had to earn our own living.

Nick. Earn it.—Is it settled about the wedding, Johnny?

Johnny. The twelfth—a week from Friday.

Linda. Why not the tenth?

Johnny. Your father had a corporation meeting.—Ushers' dinner on Monday, Nick.

Nick. *(To* Susan*)* Don't wait lunch for me Tuesday.

Susan. Just come as you are.—Oh, I gave a scream.

Linda. What's the matter?

Susan. *(To* Johnny*)* —Then you've put off your sailing, too?

Johnny. We had to.

Susan. Don't tell me it's the *Paris* now?

Johnny. Yes. Why?

Susan. But we changed ours from the tenth to the *Paris* so as not to bump into your wedding trip!

Nick. Well, we'll change back again.

Johnny. Don't think of it. It'll be great fun.

Linda. Guess what *I* did in a wild moment this morning——

Nick. What?

Linda. —Had my passport renewed—and Ned's. I want to get him away.

Susan. You're sailing then too?—It's a field-day!

Linda. No—not till a week or so after.

Johnny. Come along with us, Linda. It'd be grand. We'd own the boat.

Linda. You'll have had plenty of family by then, little man. We'll join up later.

Johnny. How long do you plan to stay over, Nick?

NICK. Oh—June—August—September—like the dirty loafers we are.

LINDA. Loafers nothing!

JOHNNY. You've got the life, you two.

LINDA. Haven't they? *(To* SUSAN*)* You know, you've always seemed to me the rightest, wisest, happiest people ever I've known.

SUSAN. Why, Linda, thanks!

LINDA. You're my one real hope in the world.

JOHNNY. Mine, too.

SUSAN. Well, when we're with a pair like you— shall I say it, Nick?

NICK. Just let them look at us: Beam, darling—

SUSAN. *(Beams)* —The Beaming Potters.

NICK. —In ten minutes of clean fun——

NICK *and* SUSAN. *(Together)* We hope you'll like us! *(Then:)*

NICK. —And what about you, Johnny? How long will you and Julia be there? *(A moment.* JOHNNY *smiles. Then:)*

JOHNNY. Well—maybe indefinitely.

LINDA. How do you mean? Julia said March.

JOHNNY. Julia doesn't know yet.

LINDA. Johnny, what *is* this?!

JOHNNY. Well, some stock that I got at about eight was kind enough to touch fifteen today. And if a deal I think's going through does go through, it'll do twice that.

SUSAN. *(Puzzled)* I must be dumb, but——

JOHNNY. Friends, there's a **very fair** chance I'll quit business next Saturday.

LINDA. Johnny!

NICK. For good?

JOHNNY. —For as long as it lasts.

SUSAN. As what lasts? Have you made some money?

JOHNNY. I think I shall have, by Saturday.

SUSAN. Good boy!

LINDA. Oh, very good boy!

NICK. —And Julia doesn't know your little plan?

JOHNNY. I haven't breathed a word of it to her.
I wanted to be sure first. It all depends on what a
Boston crowd called Bay State Power does about it.
I'll know that Monday.

LINDA. They'll do it! I don't know what it is,
but I know they'll do it! Oh, Lord, am I happy!
(A moment. Then) But, Johnny——

JOHNNY. What?

LINDA. I'm scared.

JOHNNY. Of what?

LINDA. Listen to me a moment: Father and
Julia—— *(She stops, as* SETON *and* LAURA *appear
in the doorway, and exclaims in disgust)* My God,
it's Winnie-the-Pooh! *(*JOHNNY *and* NICK *rise.*
LAURA *gazes about her.)*

LAURA. But isn't this lovely!

SETON. Well, well, so here you are! *(He comes
into the room.* LAURA *follows.)*

NICK. So we are.

SETON. Hello, Nick.—Hello, Susan!

NICK. How are you?

LAURA. *(To* SUSAN*)* My dear, what fun! We
simply never meet any more.

SUSAN. —Just a pair of parallel lines, I expect.

LAURA. I must say you're a picture, Susan.

SUSAN. *(Rises and goes to the couch)* —Madame
is in a tin bed-jacket, by Hammacher-Schlemmer.

LAURA. May we sit down a minute? *(She seats
herself in* NICK's *chair.)*

LINDA. Why not?

LAURA. I've never been up here. It's awfully
pleasant.

LINDA. We like it.

NICK. Of course, it's rather far from the car-
line——

SUSAN. And the water isn't all it might be——

NICK *and* SUSAN. *(Together)* —But *we* like it!

JOHNNY. Don't change it, friends. It's the poor man's club.

LAURA. What on earth are you all talking about?

LINDA. *(Rises and goes to the table)* Oh, just banter—airy nothings—give and take——

NICK. It's our defense against the ashman's touch.

LAURA. I *love* the decorations.

LINDA. They *love* to be loved.

LAURA. I'm afraid I don't follow you. You're not all tight, are you?

LINDA. On the continent, dear, on the continent.

NICK. We have a very high boiling-point.

SETON. *(Leans over and plucks* JOHNNY's *sleeve)* You old fox, you.

JOHNNY. Yes? How's that?

SETON. Sam Hobson's downstairs. He's just been telling me about your little haul in Seaboard. You might have let your friends in on it.

JOHNNY. There's still time. Climb aboard if you like.

SETON. I have already.—Do you know there's an order in our office to buy sixty thousand shares for Ross, of Bay State Power, all the way up to thirty?

JOHNNY. *(Quickly)* Are you sure of that?

SETON. I took the order myself.

JOHNNY. Then that cinches it.

SUSAN. Is it a real killing, Johnny?

JOHNNY. For me it is!

SETON. *(Impressively)* —Just thirty or forty thousand, that's all.

SUSAN. —No odds cents?

LINDA. Johnny—Johnny——

NICK. Let this be a lesson to you, young man.

SETON. —Anyone mind if I talk a little business? —The impression in our part of town is, it's you who put Seaboard on the map.

JOHNNY. I wouldn't go so far as that.

SETON. Ross said so himself.—Look here: we'd damn well like to have you with us, in Pritchard, Ames.

JOHNNY. Thanks, I've heard about that.

SETON. The Chief's told you already?

JOHNNY. I saw him this afternoon.

SETON. *(To* NICK*)* —To begin at twice what he gets now—and probably a directorship in Seaboard, to boot.

NICK. Well, well—to boot, eh?

SETON. *(To* JOHNNY*)* I hope you said yes.

JOHNNY. I told him I'd let him know.

SETON. Believe me when I tell you the first fifty thousand is the hardest.—It's plain sailing after that.

LINDA. *(Suddenly)* Look out, Johnny!

SETON. —In two years we'll make your forty thousand, eighty—in five, two hundred.

NICK. *(Edges over to* JOHNNY*)* —Lend a fellow a dime for a cup of coffee, mister? (JOHNNY *laughs.)*

SETON. Well, how about it?

JOHNNY. I'll let him know.

SETON. You couldn't do better than to come with us—not possibly.

JOHNNY. *(Rises and puts his glass on the table)* It's awfully nice of you, it really is.

LINDA. Look out, look *out!*

JOHNNY. Don't worry, Linda.

SETON. —Just let me give you a brief outline of the possibilities——

LINDA. That will do for business tonight, Seton.

SETON. I just want to tell Johnny——

LINDA. It's enough, really.

SETON. *(Laughs, and rises)* You're the hostess! —Then let's all go downstairs and celebrate, shall we?

LAURA. *(Rises)* Yes, let's.—It's such a wonderful party.

LINDA. I'm not going downstairs.

SETON. Oh, come along, Linda—don't be foolish.

LAURA. Do come, dear. Your father said to tell you he——

LINDA. Yes—I thought so.—But I'm not going downstairs.

NICK. *(Moves away from them to the other side of the room)* Where's the old music-box we used to play, Linda?

LINDA. Over there—but I've got something better—— *(She goes to the gramophone in the corner)* Listen—it's electric—it'll melt your heart with its——

NICK. Take it away. (SUSAN *rises.* SETON *and* LAURA *move toward the door.)*

SUSAN. Nick—you wouldn't go whimsical on us!

NICK. Oh, God, for the old scenes—the old times——

SETON. It's a quarter to twelve now, you know—

NICK. *(Is examining the music-box)* Welcome, little New Year——

LAURA. Linda, I really think that——

LINDA. I know, Laura.

NICK. *(Reads the music-box's repertory from a card)* "Sweet Marie"—"Fatal Wedding"—"Southern Roses"——

SUSAN. —And *this* is the way they used to dance when Grandmamma was a girl.

NICK. *(Covers his eyes, and gulps)* Don't. My old eyes can scarcely see for the tears.

LAURA. You're all absolutely mad.

(HENRY *and* CHARLES *enter, with a chafing-dish and a platter of cold meats. A CHORUS of male voices is heard from downstairs.)*

SUSAN. Heavens, what would that be?

LINDA. It's the Scottish Singers, the little dears— *(She is watching* JOHNNY.*)*

NICK. I wouldn't have come if I'd known the Campbells were coming—— (CHARLES *closes the door.* LINDA *starts a loud new dance-record on the gramophone.)*

SETON. *(Angrily)* What do you think this gets you, anyway?

LINDA. Peace and quiet!

NICK. *(Huddles himself in his arms)* What a night! What a night!

SUSAN. What Nick really wants is some nice beer to cry into.

LINDA. Will everybody please stop sobbing! Stop it!—Take some wine, will you, Case?

JOHNNY. Thanks.

LINDA. *(Intensely)* If you weaken now—!

JOHNNY. I never felt stronger.

LINDA. *(Turns to* SUSAN*)* Peter and Mary—they couldn't have ditched us, could they?

SUSAN. Oh, no, they'll be along——

NICK. Eleven forty-seven—what *can* be keeping old Doctor Stork? (HENRY *and* CHARLES, *having placed the platter and chafing-dish upon the table, go out.)*

LAURA. *(At the door)* Linda—really—people are beginning to wonder a little——

LINDA. I am *not going downstairs.*

LAURA. *(Laughs unpleasantly)* Well, of course, if——

LINDA. But I wouldn't dream of keeping anyone who wants to——

LAURA. *(Stares a moment, then turns to* SETON*)* Apparently we aren't welcome here.

SETON. I gathered that some time ago.—Linda, I think your conduct toward your guests tonight is **outrageous.**

LAURA. And so do I.

LINDA. I imagined that was what brought you up, you sweet things.

SETON. If you ask me, it's one of the worst cases of downright rudeness I've ever seen.

LINDA. And has someone asked you?

LAURA. —When a girl invites three hundred people to her house, and then proceeds to——

LINDA. I invited six people—three of whom you see before you. The others came on someone else's say-so—yours and Father's, I believe.

LAURA. Perhaps we'd better go home, Seton.

LINDA. Oh, you're here now. Stay, if you like. I'd prefer it, however, if you'd do your commenting on my behavior not to my face, but behind my back as usual——

LAURA. *(Opens the door)* Come, Seton—— *(She goes out, with all the hauteur she can command.)*

SETON. *(To* LINDA*)* When I think of the——

LINDA. —Before you go, you wouldn't care to swing on the old trapeze a while, would you—? *(He stares. She turns away)* I suppose not. *(*SETON *goes out, closing the door after him.* LINDA *moves toward the table)* Oh, the cheek, the cheek!

NICK. Some day they'll draw themselves up like that and won't be able to get down again. *(He goes to* JOHNNY*)* Well, Johnny——!

JOHNNY. *(At the table)* Lord, it's the grandest feeling—— Oh, wait till Julia hears! On tonight of all nights, too! What a break that is!

LINDA. I've never been so happy for anyone in my life.

NICK. Go to it, boy!

JOHNNY. Oh, won't I? Watch me! *(Then)* —Where'll we spend the Spring?—Let's all spend the Spring together!

NICK. What do you say, Susan? Do you think we could stand them?

SUSAN. There'll always be a curse and a blow for you with us, Johnny.

LINDA. Can I come? Please, can I come, too—? *(She trots in among them.)*

NICK. Don't leave us, darling. We want you. We need you. (SUSAN *joins them. She sits at the end of the table, opposite* NICK, *and* JOHNNY *and* LINDA *behind it, facing the front.* JOHNNY *refills the glasses and* SUSAN *and* LINDA *serve the food.)*

SUSAN. How about the south.of France?

JOHNNY. Why not?

LINDA. No, no—the air reeks of roses and the nightingales make the nights hideous.

JOHNNY. *(Overcome)* Don't—don't—— *(He gives each of them a glass of wine.)*

NICK. *(A suggestion)* If we went to Norway, we could all paint a house at midnight.

JOHNNY. —Norway's out. It's got to be some place you can swim all day long.—You know, it's just dawned on me that I've never swum enough. That's one of the things I want to do: *swim.*

NICK. *(Rises and leans upon the table)* Young man, in the bright lexicon of youth there is no such word. Swimming is for idlers.

SUSAN. —And Hawaiians.

LINDA. —And fish.

NICK. Are you a fish? Answer me that.—Can you look yourself squarely in the eye and say "I am a fish"? No. You cannot.

JOHNNY. You are a hard man, sir.

NICK. It is life that has made me hard, son.

JOHNNY. —But I want only to be like you, Daddy —how can I be like you?

NICK. You ask me for the story of my success? —Well, I'll tell you——

LINDA. Come—gather close, **children.** *(They turn their chairs and face him.)*

NICK. —I arrived in this country at the age of three months, with nothing in my pockets but five cents and an old hat-check. I had no friends, little or no education, and sex to me was still the Great Mystery. But when I came down the gang-plank of that little sailing-vessel—steam was then unknown, except to the very rich—— Friends, can you picture that manly little figure without a tug at your heart strings, and a faint wave of nausea? But I just pulled my belt a little tighter, and told myself, "Don't forget you're a Potter, Nick"—I called myself "Nick"—and so I found myself at my first job, in the glass works. Glass was in its infancy then—we had barely scratched the surface—but I have never shirked work—and if there was an errand to be run, I ran five errands. If someone wanted to get off at the third floor, I took him to the tenth floor.—Then one day came my big chance. I was in the glass-blowing department then—now Miss Murphy's department—and a very capable little woman she is——

LINDA. Why, Mr. Potter, I'm no such thing.

NICK. Oh, yes, you are, Miss Murphy! Well, sir, I was blowing glass like a two-year-old, whistling as I blew. Suddenly I looked down and found in my hand—*a bottle*—or what we now know as a bottle. I rushed to my employer, a Mr. Grandgent, and said, "Look, Mr. Grandgent—I think I've got something here." Mr. Grandgent looked—and laughed—*laughed,* do you understand?—I went from city to city like some hunted thing, that laugh still in my ears. But with me went my bottle. They called it Potter's Folly. They said it would never work. Well, time has shown how right they were. Now the bottle is in every home. I have made the bottle a National Institution!—And that, my dears, is how I met your grandmother. *(He bows.)*

LINDA. *(Rises, champagne-glass in hand)* —To one who, in the face of every difficulty, has proved himself a Christian gentleman.—Music, music! *(She goes to the gramophone and starts a record.)*

SUSAN. *(Rises)* —To one who has been friend to rich and poor alike——

JOHNNY. *(Rises)* —To one who, as soldier——

LINDA. —As statesman——

SUSAN. —As navigator——

JOHNNY. —As man about town——

LINDA. —As scout-leader——

NICK. —As Third Vice-President of the second largest spat factory in East St. Louis——

JOHNNY. On behalf of the hook-and-ladder company of the First Reformed Church, I want to say a few words about our brave Fire Laddies. Has it occurred to you—— *(The door opens and JULIA and EDWARD enter.)*

EDWARD. Linda!

LINDA. Yes?

EDWARD. Please turn that machine off. *(SUSAN goes to NICK.)*

LINDA. You know Mr. and Mrs. Potter, Father——

EDWARD. *(Curtly)* How do you do? *(Then to LINDA)* Turn it off, Linda—— *(LINDA stops the record.)*

NICK. *(To SUSAN)* —Fell, or was pushed.

JOHNNY. *(Moves eagerly toward JULIA)* Julia! Listen, darling! I've got a grand surprise for you—

EDWARD. Just a moment!—You must all come down, now. It's nearly twelve, and we want the entire party together to see the New Year in.

LINDA. But there are two parties, Father—the one down there and mine—*here.*

EDWARD. Please do as I say, Linda.

LINDA. I asked for permission to have a few

of my friends here tonight. You said I might. I've got some of them, now, and——

EDWARD. —I noticed you had.

LINDA. —And more are coming.

JULIA. They've come, haven't they?

LINDA. How do you mean?

JULIA. Peter Jessup and what's-her-name—Mary Hedges——

LINDA. What about them?

JULIA. They're downstairs.

LINDA. They—?—How long have they been there?

JULIA. Twenty minutes or so. I said you'd be down.

LINDA. Oh, you did, did you?

JULIA. —They're being very amusing. I said we expected them to be. Jessup has done his trained-seal act to perfection, and now I think Mary Hedges is about to give her imitations. *(There is a silence. LINDA stares at her, speechless.)* They're a great success, really.

LINDA. *(Without turning)* Nick—will you and Susan bring them up to my sitting-room? I'll be there in a minute.

SUSAN. All right, Linda. *(She moves toward the door. NICK follows, gazing anxiously at the ceiling as he goes.)*

NICK. —The New Year ought to be just about passing over Stamford. *(They go out, closing the door after them.)*

JOHNNY. *(Goes to JULIA)* Julia! Big news, dear —guess what's happened?

LINDA. *(To EDWARD and JULIA, before JULIA can reply)* Oh, this is so humiliating.—Peter and Mary are my guests, do you understand? Not paid entertainers—— *(She moves away from them.)*

JULIA. I'm sorry. I simply couldn't imagine mixing in people like that to no purpose.

LINDA. Couldn't you?

JULIA. No.—But of course I can't follow your reasoning these days, Linda. I can't follow it at all.

EDWARD. *(To* LINDA*)* There's no cause for temper, child. Just run along now, and we'll follow. Julia and I want to talk to Johnny for a moment.

JULIA. *(Turns again to* JOHNNY*)* What is it, Johnny? Quick, tell me!

LINDA. —Listen to me, Father: tonight means a good deal to me—I don't know what, precisely—and I don't know how. Something is trying to take it away from me, and I can't let it go. I'll put in an appearance downstairs, if you like. Then I want to bring a few people up here—the few people in the world I can talk to, and feel something for. And I want to sit with them and have supper with them, and we won't disturb anyone. That's all right with you, isn't it?

EDWARD. Your place is downstairs.

LINDA. Once more, Father: this is important to me. Don't ask me why. I don't know. It has something to do with—when I was a child here—and this room—and good times in it—and——

EDWARD. What special virtue this room has, I'm sure I don't see.

LINDA. You don't, do you—no—you can't. Well, I'll tell you this room's my home. It's the only home I've got. There's something here that I understand, and that understands me. Maybe it's Mother.

EDWARD. Please do as I have told you, Linda.

LINDA. I suppose you know it's the end of us, then.

EDWARD. Don't talk nonsense. Do as I say.

LINDA. It *is* the end. But all the same, I'm going to have supper here tonight in my home with my friends.

EDWARD. I have told you——

LINDA. —You thought I'd come around, didn't
you? You always think people will come around.
Not me: not tonight. And I shan't be bothered here,
either. Because if there's one thing you can't stand
it's a scene. I can promise you one, if you inter-
fere. I can promise you a beauty. (EDWARD *turns
from her.* LINDA *looks about her, at the room.)*

EDWARD. —Well, Johnny, so there's good news,
is there?

LINDA. *(Suddenly)* Was Mother a sweet soul,
Father? Was she exciting?

EDWARD. *(To* JOHNNY) —A happy day all
around, eh? An engagement to be announced, New
Year's to celebrate—and now——

LINDA. Was Mother a sweet soul, Father? Was
she exciting?

EDWARD. Your mother was a very beautiful and
distinguished woman. *(To* JOHNNY) Naturally, I
am delighted that——

LINDA. Was she a sweet soul, Father? Was she
exciting? *(For an instant* EDWARD *loses control of
himself.)*

EDWARD. Linda, if you are not happy here, why
don't you go away? I should be glad if next month
you would take your maid and Miss Talcott and go
on a trip somewhere. You distress me. You cause
nothing but trouble and upsets. You——

LINDA. All right, Father. That's just what I'm
going to do, after the wedding. No maid and no
Miss Talcott, though. Just me—Linda—the kid
herself——

EDWARD. As you wish.

LINDA. I've wanted to get out for years. I've
never known it so well as tonight. I can't bear it
here any longer. It's doing terrible things to me.

EDWARD. —And will you leave this room now,
please?

LINDA. This room—this room—I don't think

you'll be able to stand it long. I'll come back when
you've left it—— *(She goes out. There is a silence.
Then:)*

JULIA. She's dreadful tonight. She's made one
situation after another.

EDWARD. Never mind, my dear. Things will
settle themselves. *(He seats himself in a chair at
Right)* Well, Johnny—I don't think I need worry
about the way *you'll* take care of Julia, need I?

JOHNNY. *(Laughs, uncertainly)* We'll try to
manage!

EDWARD. I consider what you've done a fine piece
of work. I congratulate you.

JULIA. Oh, and so do I—so do *I*, dear! *(She
sits near her father.)*

JOHNNY. —But you don't know yet, do you?

EDWARD. The fact is, Seton has just now told us.

JULIA. Isn't it marvelous?—Oh, what a New
Year!

EDWARD. —Your stock is going up with a rush,
it seems. It's time to make hay, I think.

JOHNNY. Hay?

EDWARD. *(With relish)* Money! Money!

JULIA. *Now* all those years you worked so hard
—they'll pay interest now, Johnny! *(The frown
grows between* JOHNNY'S *eyes.)*

EDWARD. Of course, I could put you into the
Bank tomorrow—but I am not sure that that would
be advisable at present.

JULIA. —That will come, won't it, Johnny? *(To
EDWARD)* You'd better not wait *too* long, though—
he may cost you too much!

EDWARD. *(Smiles)* We'll have to risk that. People always do. *(Then seriously)* Pritchard, Ames
is an excellent house. In my opinion, you could not
do better than to go with them. Then, in five or six
years, you come to us on your own merit. After
that, as the children put it, "the sky's the limit."

You're in a fair way to be a man of means at forty-
five. I'm proud of you.

JOHNNY. *(There is a pause. Finally)* But—I'd
made up my mind not to take the Pritchard, Ames
offer.

EDWARD. What? And why not?

JOHNNY. I don't want to get tied up for life quite
so soon. You see, I'm a kind of a queer duck, in a
way. I'm afraid I'm not as anxious as I might be
for the things most people work toward. I don't
want too much money.

EDWARD. Too *much* money?

JOHNNY. Well, more than I need to live by. *(He
seats himself facing them and begins eagerly, hope-
fully, to tell them his plan)* —You see, it's always
been my plan to make a few thousands early in the
game, if I could, and then quit for as long as they
last, and try to find out who I am and what I am
and what goes on and what about it—now, while
I'm young, and feel good all the time.—I'm sure Julia
understands what I'm getting at—don't you, Julia?

JULIA. *(Laughs, uncertainly)* I'm not sure I do,
Johnny!

EDWARD. You wish to occupy yourself otherwise,
is that it?—with some—er—art or other, say——

JOHNNY. Oh, no, I've got no abilities that way.
I'm not one of the frail ones with a longing to get
away from it all and indulge a few tastes, either.
I haven't any tastes. Old china and first editions
and gate-legged tables don't do a thing to me. I
don't want to live any way or in any time but my
own—now—in New York—and Detroit—and Chi-
cago—and Phoenix—any place here—but I do want
to live!

EDWARD. —As a gentleman of leisure.

JOHNNY. —As a man whose time, for a while at
least, is his own. That's what I've been plugging

for ever since I was ten. Please don't make me feel guilty about it, sir. Whether I'm right or wrong, it's more important to me than anything in the world but Julia. Even if it turns out to be just one of those fool ideas that people dream about and then go flat on—even if I find I've had enough of it in three months, still I want it. I've got a feeling that if I let this chance go by, there'll never be another for me. So I don't think anyone will mind if I—just have a go at it—will they, Julia? (JULIA *is silent.*) —Will they, dear? (JULIA *rises.* JOHNNY *rises with her.*)

JULIA. *(After a moment)* Father—wi'l you let Johnny and me talk a while?

EDWARD. Just a moment—— *(He rises and turns to* JOHNNY*)* —As I understand it, you have some objection, perhaps, to our manner of living——

JOHNNY. Not for you, sir. I haven't the slightest doubt it's all right for you—or that it's the answer for a lot of people. But for me—well, you see I don't *want* to live in what they call "a certain way." In the first place I'd be no good at it and besides that I don't want to be identified with any one class of people. I want to live every whichway, among all kinds—and know them—and understand them—and love them—*that's* what I want!—Don't you, Julia?

JULIA. Why, I—— It sounds——

EDWARD. In all my experience, I have never heard such a——

JOHNNY. I want these years now, sir.

JULIA. Father—please—— *(He turns to her. Their eyes meet.)* —It will be all right, I promise you.

EDWARD. *(Moves toward the door, where he turns once more to* JOHNNY*)* Case, it strikes me that you chose a strange time to tell us this, a very strange time.

JOHNNY. *(Puzzled)* I don't quite——

EDWARD. —In fact, if I had not already sent the announcement to the newspapers—asked a number of our friends here tonight to——

JULIA. Father!

JOHNNY. *(Very quietly)* Oh, I see.

JULIA. Father—please go down. We'll come in a minute. (EDWARD *hesitates an instant, then goes out.)*

JOHNNY. *(Still hopeful, turns to* JULIA*)* —Darling, he didn't get what I'm driving at, at all! My plan is——

JULIA. Oh, Johnny, Johnny, why did you do it?

JOHNNY. Do what?

JULIA. You knew how all that talk would antagonize him.

JOHNNY. *(A moment)* You think talk is all it was?

JULIA. I think it was less than that! I'm furious with you.

JOHNNY. It wasn't just talk, Julia.

JULIA. Well, if you think you can persuade me that a man of your energy and your ability possibly *could* quit at thirty for *any* length of time, you're mistaken.

JOHNNY. I'd like a try at it.

JULIA. It's ridiculous—and why you chose tonight of all nights to go on that way to Father——

JOHNNY. Wait a minute, dear: we'd better get clear on this——

JULIA. I'm clear on it now! If you're tired, and need a holiday, we'll have it. We'll take two months instead of one, if you like. We'll——

JOHNNY. That wouldn't settle anything.

JULIA. Johnny, I've known quite a few men who don't work—and of all the footling, unhappy existences—it's inconceivable that you could stand it—it's unthinkable you could!

JOHNNY. —I might do it differently.

JULIA. Differently!

JOHNNY. *(A moment. Then)* Julia, do you love me? *(She looks at him swiftly, then looks away.)*

JULIA. *(Lowly)* You—you have a great time standing me against a wall and throwing knives around me, don't you? *(In an instant he has taken her in his arms.)*

JOHNNY. Oh, sweet——

JULIA. *(Against his shoulder)* What do you do things like that for? What's the matter with you, anyway?

JOHNNY. *(He stands off and looks at her)* Haven't you the remotest idea of what I'm after? *(She looks at him, startled.)* I'm after—all that's in me, all I am. I want to get it out—where I can look at it, know it. That takes time.—Can't you understand that?

JULIA. But you haven't an idea yet of how exciting *business* can be—you're just beginning! Oh, Johnny, see it through! You'll love it. I know you will. There's no such thrill in the world as making money. It's the most—what are you staring at?

JOHNNY. Your face.

JULIA. *(She turns away)* Oh—you won't listen to me—you won't hear me——

JOHNNY. Yes, I will.

JULIA. *(A pause. Then JULIA speaks in another voice)* And you'd expect me to live on—this money you've made, too, would you?

JOHNNY. Why, of course not. You have all you'll ever need for anything you'd want, haven't you?

JULIA. *(Another pause, then)* —I suppose it doesn't occur to you how badly it would *look* for you to stop now, does it——?

JOHNNY. Look? How? *(She does not answer.)* —Oh—you mean there'd be those who'd think I'd married money and called it a day——

JULIA. There would be. There'd be plenty of them.

JOHNNY. —And you'd mind that, would you?

JULIA. Well, I'm not precisely anxious to have it thought of you.

JOHNNY. —Because *I* shouldn't mind it—and I think that lookout's mine. Oh, darling, you don't see what I'm aiming at, either—but try a little blind faith for a while, won't you? Come along with me——

JULIA. Johnny—— *(She reaches for his hand.)*

JOHNNY. —The whole way, dear.

JULIA. —Wait till next year—or two years, and we'll think about it again. If it's right, it can be done, then as well as now.—You can do that for me —for us—can't you? *(A moment. Then he slowly brings her around and looks into her eyes.)*

JOHNNY. You think by then I'd have "come around." That's what you think, isn't it?—I'd have "come around"——

JULIA. But surely you can at least see that if—! *(She stops, as* LINDA *re-enters.)*

LINDA. It lacks six minutes of the New Year, if anyone's interested. *(A moment, then* JULIA *moves toward the door.)*

JULIA. Come on, Johnny.

JOHNNY. *(To* LINDA*)* Where are the others?

LINDA. My pretty new friends? Well, it seems they've ditched me. *(She starts a tune on the music-box)* —This won't make too much noise, do you think?

JOHNNY. How do you mean, Linda?

LINDA. I imagine Peter and Mary got tired of being put through their tricks, and slid out when they could. Nick and Susan left a message upstairs with Delia saying that they had to go after them. I'm supposed to follow, but I don't think I will, somehow.

JULIA. Oh, I *am* sorry.

LINDA. Are you, Julia? That's a help. *(She goes to the supper-table)* —Anyone care for a few cold cuts before the fun starts?

JOHNNY. You're not going to stay up here all alone——

LINDA. Why not? I'm just full of resources. I crack all kinds of jokes with myself—and they say the food's good. *(She takes a bite of a sandwich and puts it down again)* Ugh! Kiki——

JULIA. Linda, this is plain stubbornness, and you know it.

LINDA. *(Wheels about sharply)* Listen, Julia—! *(She stops, and turns away)* No—that gets you nowhere, does it?

JULIA. *(To JOHNNY)* Are you coming?

JOHNNY. I think I'll wait a moment with Linda, if you don't mind.

JULIA. But I do mind!—Will you come, please?

JOHNNY. —In a moment, Julia. *(JULIA looks at him. He meets her gaze steadily. She turns and goes out. There is a pause. Then:)*

LINDA. You'd better run on down, don't you think?

JOHNNY. Not right away *(Another pause.)*

LINDA. I'm afraid I don't know how to entertain you. I've done all my stuff.

JOHNNY. I don't need entertaining.

LINDA. *(Another pause, a very long one. LINDA looks uncertainly toward the music-box. Finally)* —You wouldn't care to step into a waltz, Mr. Case?

JOHNNY. I'd love it. *(She extends her arms. He takes her in his. They begin to waltz slowly to the music-box.)* —There's a conspiracy against you and me, child.

LINDA. What's that?

JOHNNY. The Vested Interests——

LINDA. I know.

JOHNNY. —They won't let you have any fun, and they won't give me time to think.

LINDA. I suppose, like the great fathead you **are**, you told them all your little hopes and dreams.

JOHNNY. Um.

LINDA. —Pretty disappointing?

JOHNNY. Bad enough.

LINDA. Poor boy.

JOHNNY. How about your own evening?

LINDA. Not so good, either.

JOHNNY. Poor girl.

LINDA. But we won't mind, will we?

JOHNNY. Hell, no, we won't mind.

LINDA. We'll get there——

JOHNNY. We'll get there! *(She stops in the dance and looks up at him for a moment, curiously. Then he smiles at her and she smiles back.)*

JOHNNY. —Place head, A, against cheek, B, and proceed as before—— *(They begin to dance again.)* —Of course they may be right.

LINDA. Don't you believe it!

JOHNNY. They seem—awfully sure.

LINDA. It's your ride still, isn't it? You know where you want to go, don't you?

JOHNNY. Well, I thought I did.

LINDA. So did I.—Pathetic, wasn't it—all my fuss and fury over anything so unimportant as this party.

JOHNNY. Maybe it was important.

LINDA. Well, if it was, I'm not. And I guess that's the answer.

JOHNNY. Not quite.

LINDA. —Me and my little what-do-you-call-it— defense mechanism—so pathetic. Yes, I'm just chock-full of pathos, I am.

JOHNNY. You're a brick, Linda.

LINDA. Oh, shut your silly face—— *(Then)* You're right, you know—there *is* nothing up the fun-alley.

JOHNNY. Fun-alley?

LINDA. I had a nice little seven-word motto for my life, but I guess she don't work——

JOHNNY. What was it?

LINDA. "Not very important—but pretty good entertainment."

JOHNNY. H'm——

LINDA. For "pretty good" read "rotten." *(They dance for a few moments, silently. Then* LINDA *stops)* There. That's enough. I'm getting excited.

JOHNNY. —What?

LINDA. —It was grand. Thanks. You can go now. *(She has not yet left his arms. Suddenly from outside comes the sound of BELLS tolling. Her grasp tightens upon his arm)* Listen! *(She looks over her shoulder toward the window. HORNS begin to be heard from the distance, long-drawn-out, insistent.)*

JOHNNY. It's it, all right.

LINDA. *(Again she turns her face to his)* Happy New Year, Johnny.

JOHNNY. *(He bends and kisses her)* Happy New Year, dear. *(For an instant she clings to him, then averts her face.)*

LINDA. *(In a breath)* Oh, Johnny, you're so attractive——

JOHNNY. *(With difficulty)* You're—you're all right yourself—— *(There is a dead silence. Then she leaves his arms, turns and smiles to him.)*

LINDA. —You can count on Sister Linda.—Run on down now—quick! They'll be waiting.

JOHNNY. *(Hesitates)* Linda——

LINDA. What?

JOHNNY. They've—your father—I've been put in a position that——

LINDA. Do you love Julia, Johnny? *(He turns away.)*

JOHNNY. Of course I do.

(NED *enters silently, another glass in hand. He stands in the shadow at Left, watching them, swaying almost imperceptibly.*)

LINDA. —Well, if ever she needed you, she needs you now. Once it's announced she'll go through with it. Then you can help her. I can't do anything any more. I've tried for twenty years. You're all that's left. Go on, Johnny—— *(He goes to the door. From downstairs a swelling CHORUS of male voices begins Auld Lang Syne.)* —And tell those choir-boys for me that I'll be in Scotland before them.

(JOHNNY *goes out, closing the door after him. LINDA stops the music-box, then moves slowly to the window, Right, where she stands silently for a moment, looking out. NED is still watching her, immobile. At length she turns to him:*)

LINDA. —Just take any place, Ned. *(He goes to the couch and sits there.)*
NED. —Rum party down there, isn't it?
LINDA. A hundred million dollars knocking together never made many sparks that I could see. *(She takes a glass of wine from the table)* What's it like to get drunk, Ned?
NED. It's—— How drunk?
LINDA. Good and drunk.
NED. Grand.
LINDA. *(She seats herself near the table, facing him)* How is it?
NED. Well, to begin with, it brings you to life.
LINDA. Does it?
NED. Yes.—And after a little while you begin to

know all about it. You feel—I don't know—important——

LINDA. That must be good.

NED. It is.—Then pretty soon the game starts.

LINDA. What game?

NED. —That you play with yourself. It's a swell
game—there's not a sweller game on this earth,
really——

LINDA. *(Sips her wine)* How does it go?

NED. Well, you think clear as crystal, but every
move, every sentence is a problem. That—gets
pretty interesting.

LINDA. I see.

NED. Swell game. Most terribly exciting game.

LINDA. You—get beaten, though, don't you?

NED. Sure. But that's good, too. Then you don't
mind anything—not anything at all. Then you sleep.

LINDA. *(She is watching him, fascinated)* How
—long can you keep it up?

NED. A long while. As long as you last.

LINDA. Oh, Ned—that's awful!

NED. Think so?—Other things are worse.

LINDA. But—but where do you end up?

NED. Where does everybody end up? You die.
—And that's all right, too.

LINDA. *(A pause. Then)* Ned, can you do it on
champagne?

NED. Why—— *(He stops and looks at her, in-
tently)* —What's the matter, Linda?

LINDA. *(She finishes her glass and sets it down)*
Nothing.

NED. I know.

LINDA. Yes?

NED. Johnny.

LINDA. Give me some more wine, Ned.

NED. *(Rises and goes over to her)* He's a funny
guy, isn't he?

LINDA. Give me some, Ned——

NED. *(He goes to the table, refills her glass, returns, and gives it to her)* —You can tell me about it, dear.

LINDA. *(Looks up at him. A moment, then)* I love the boy, Neddy.

NED. I thought so.—Hell, isn't it?

LINDA. I guess it will be. *(Warn CURTAIN.)*

NED. *(Raises his glass)* Here's luck to you——

LINDA. *(Stares at her glass)* I don't want any luck. (NED *moves away from her to the table near the couch. He finishes his drink, leaves it there and sinks down upon the couch.* LINDA *carefully sets her glass of wine, untouched, upon the supper table, and rises)* I think what I'd better do is—— *(She moves slowly to the door, and opens it. The SONG is just finishing. It is APPLAUDED.* LINDA *hesitates at the door)* Ned—— *(He does not answer. Suddenly, from downstairs, comes a long roll of DRUMS.* LINDA *stiffens. She starts to close the door, but is held there, her hand upon the knob.* EDWARD'S *VOICE begins to be heard:)*

EDWARD. Ladies and gentlemen—my very good friends: I have the honor to announce to you the engagement of my daughter, Julia, to Mr. John Case —an event which doubles the pleasure I take in wishing you—and them—a most happy and prosperous New Year. *(There is prolonged APPLAUSE and through it CONGRATULATIONS and LAUGHTER. Slowly she closes the door, but still stands with her hand upon it. Finally she speaks, without turning:)*

LINDA. Ned—*(He does not answer.)* Ned— maybe I ought to go down and—I'm not sure I *will* stay up here—do you mind? *(He is silent. She turns and sees him)* Ned! *(He is asleep. She goes to him swiftly, speaking again, in a low voice)* Ned—— *(A moment. Then)* Poor lamb. *(She bends and kisses him. She goes to the doorway, turns off the LIGHTS in the Playroom, and opens the door. A confusion of excited VOICES is heard from downstairs. In the lighted hallway* LINDA *turns to the stairs, raises her head and goes out, calling above the voices)* Hello!—Hello, everyone!

CURTAIN

ACT THREE

SCENE: *The same as Act I.*

TIME: *Twelve days later. Ten o'clock at night.*
The curtains are drawn and the lamps lighted.
Coffee service is on a small table near the fire-
place. NICK *and* SUSAN *are taking their coffee.*
LINDA'S *cup is on the table. She stands near the*
sofa at Left Center, frowning at NICK.

LINDA. No?

NICK. *(Shakes his head)* Not possibly. *(He is*
behind the sofa at Right, upon which SUSAN *is*
seated.)

SUSAN. Why should Johnny pick a place like
that?

LINDA. Why should he go away at all?

NICK. I'd have done the same thing—I'd have
just giv' 'er a look, I would, and flounced out.

SUSAN. Hush, Nick. This is no time for fooling.

LINDA. *(Thinks a minute, then head down, eyes*
on the floor, she paces across the room and back, and
cross again. She stops opposite them and turns)
—Atlantic City.

SUSAN. You don't go to Atlantic City for six
days to think.

NICK. Old Chinese proverb.

LINDA. But where can he be, then?—*Where?*

SUSAN. Don't worry, Linda. I'm sure he's all
right.

NICK. Susan and I parted forever at least forty times. *(To* SUSAN*)* —Or was it forty-seven?

SUSAN. Of course.—And they haven't even done that. They've just put off the wedding a while.

LINDA. I know, but—— *(She looks away, anxiously)* Oh, Lordy, Lordy——

NICK. Johnny will come around, Linda. He's up against the old fight between spirit and matter—anyone want to take a hundred on spirit?

LINDA. I will! I'll take two hundred!

NICK. It's a bet, Madam. *(He looks at his watch.)*

SUSAN. Don't forget we have to go back to the house for our bags, Nick.

NICK. There's lots of time. She doesn't sail until midnight. "She"—a boat that size, "she"—the big nance. *(To* LINDA*)* —You don't really want to see us off, do you?

LINDA. Oh, yes! But can you stop back for me on your way down?

SUSAN. If you like.

LINDA. I don't want to leave here till the last minute. I keep feeling that something may happen.

SUSAN. Where's Julia now?

LINDA. She went to dine some place with Father. He won't let her out of his sight—or into mine.

NICK. No wonder Johnny took to the woods.

LINDA. *(Quickly)* —The woods?

NICK. —Or wherever he did take to.

LINDA. Now I know!

SUSAN. Yes?

LINDA. It was at Placid they met. It was at Placid they—of course! *(She goes to the telephone behind the sofa, at Left.)*

NICK. *(To* SUSAN*)* It may be. They say they always return to the scene of the crime.

LINDA. Long distance, please.

SUSAN. —In which case, I suppose Julia wins.

NICK. I don't know. It's pretty cold at Placid.

There's nothing for a rapid pulse like a little wet snow up the sleeve.

LINDA. Long distance, please——

SUSAN. *(To* NICK*)* Would you mind telling me how a man like Johnny is attracted to a girl like that, in the first place?

NICK. *(To* SUSAN*)* You're too young to know, Susan.

LINDA. *(At the telephone)* —Long distance?

SUSAN. I can think of several people who'd be better for Johnny than Julia.

LINDA. I want to speak with Lake Placid, New York——

NICK. I can think of one, anyway.

LINDA. —Placid—the Lake Placid Club.

SUSAN. Do you suppose she's in love with him?

NICK. Suppose? I know. Look at her.

LINDA. "P-l-a-c-i-d"——

NICK. Tiger, Tiger, Tiger.

LINDA. Quiet a minute, will you? *(To the telephone)* —Placid—calm—peaceful. Yes. And I'd like to speak with Mr. John Case.

SUSAN. If I could grab you the way I did, she can——

NICK. But there's more in this than meets the ear, darling—Julia.

LINDA. Quiet! *(Then, to the telephone)* —Miss Seton. *Linda* Seton. *(To* SUSAN*)* —I don't want to give him heart-failure, thinking it's—— *(To the telephone)* —John Case—Lake Placid Club—Linda Seton. Thanks. *(She replaces the receiver and returns to* NICK *and* SUSAN*)* I'm sure he's there. I feel it in my bones.

NICK. *(A pause. Then)* Linda, Johnny asked me not to tell anyone, but I think you ought to know something: the fact is, he's got a single cabin on the *Paris* for himself tonight.

LINDA. He——? How do you know?

NICK. Because I got it for him.

LINDA. You don't seriously think he'd do it?

NICK. No—I can't say I do.

LINDA. Well, *I* do! Oh, Lord—then he's in New York now!

NICK. Maybe so.

LINDA. He can't be, or he'd be here.—Where did he go to, Nick?

NICK. —Of that, I wasn't informed.

LINDA. You know, this is ageing me.

SUSAN. We know something else you don't know, Linda.

LINDA. Oh! What is it?

NICK. —Look out, Susan. Steady, girl.

LINDA. *(Glances at them quickly, then lights a cigarette)* What is it?

SUSAN. How did you happen to decide not to come abroad, as you planned?

LINDA. Why, I—well, I thought probably Johnny and Julia—they'd rather not have any family tagging along, and besides that, I want to get Ned off on a trip with me—out West, if I can.

SUSAN. I know. But——

NICK. *(Again NICK cuts across her)* —I saw Ned in Jimmy's last night. He was—well, if I may use the word——

SUSAN. Look here, Linda——

LINDA. *(To NICK)* —I think he's all right tonight. He went to a show with the Wheelers.

NICK. *(Reflects)* I wonder if they're really in love with each other.

LINDA. They're terribly in love.

SUSAN. What makes you think so?

LINDA. I know it. Johnny couldn't help but be, and Julia——

SUSAN. *(Glances at NICK)* You meant the Wheelers, didn't you?

NICK. Why, I—yes, I did.

LINDA. I don't know about them. *(She moves away from them, then back again.)*

SUSAN. Can't *you* do anything with her, Linda?

LINDA. Who—Julia?

SUSAN. Yes.

LINDA. I've talked myself blue in the face. It's no good. She won't listen. I've had the cold-shoulder and the deaf-ear so long now I'm all hoarse and half frozen.

SUSAN. I thought she's always depended on you.

LINDA. Well, she doesn't any more.

SUSAN. You love her a great deal, don't you?

LINDA. *(Laughs shortly)* I expect I do!

SUSAN. —But my dear child, don't you see that if she thinks just as your father does——

LINDA. Johnny'll fix that. Johnny'll fix everything.

SUSAN. He'll never change *them*, Linda.

LINDA. Susan, you don't know that man.

NICK. —It'd be a pity to deprive your father of the pleasure he'd take in putting him over on the town.

LINDA. Don't speak of it. That's one thing Johnny's been spared so far. I don't think he's had an inkling of *it* yet.

NICK. It will come: Mr. and Mrs. John Sebastian Case have closed their Sixty-fourth Street house and gone to Coney Island for the hunting. Mrs. Case will be remembered as Julia Seton, of Seton Pretty.

SUSAN. I'd like a picture of him, when it happens.

NICK. I wouldn't.

LINDA. —If they'd only listen to me—I've got to make them listen!—And he's so sweet, he's so attractive. What's the matter with the girl, anyway? She ought to know by now that men like Johnny don't grow on every bush.

SUSAN. —But you see, the things you like in him are just what she can't stand, Linda. And the fate you say he'll save her from is the one fate in this whole world she wants.

LINDA. I don't believe it.—Even so, she loves him —and there's been a break—and wouldn't you think she'd at least be woman enough to hang on—*hang on!*

SUSAN. I don't know. There's another who isn't woman enough to grab.

LINDA. *(There is a silence. Finally* LINDA *speaks)* —I don't quite get you, Susan.

SUSAN. Well, to make it plain, no man's lost this side of the altar.

NICK. She's talking a lot of—— *(Then, to* SU-SAN*)* Come on, Pearl—ups-a-daisy.

LINDA. Susan——

SUSAN. Yes, dear?

LINDA. Julia has never in her life loved anyone but Johnny.

SUSAN. —And you.

LINDA. —And me.

NICK. *(In spite of himself)* —And herself.

LINDA. *(Turns on him sharply)* That's not true! —Even in this it's of him she's thinking—she may be mistaken, but it *is* of him!

SUSAN. I've no doubt she believes that.

LINDA. Well, I believe it too!

NICK. —Come on, will you, Susan?

LINDA. I think it's rotten of you to suspect things of Julia that aren't Julia at all, and I think it's worse of you to——

NICK. We're sorry, Linda, really we are.

LINDA. You aren't sorry! You're—— *(Sudden-ly she covers her face with her hands)* Oh, what's the matter with me?

SUSAN. Linda, I could shake you.

LINDA. I wish you would.—I wish someone would, till there was nothing left to shake.

SUSAN. —And there's not a thing to do about it?

LINDA. What there is to do, I'm doing. *(She goes to the window at Back. A silence. Then:)*

SUSAN. —And if you did anything else, I expect you wouldn't be Linda.

NICK. Linda, I think you're just about the—— *(But that is as close as he can get to a declaration of faith)* —Oh, hell—— *(He turns to* SUSAN*)* Will you come, dear? It's ten-thirty.

SUSAN. *(Rises and moves toward* LINDA. NICK *follows)* But if Johnny should—— *(*LINDA *faces her.)* —Promise us one thing, Linda.

LINDA. What?

SUSAN. *(After a moment)* Nothing.

LINDA. I love you two.

SUSAN. —And so do we love you.

LINDA. —Call back for me when?

SUSAN. In half an hour.

NICK. Less.

LINDA. —Then could your car possibly take me out to Mary Hedges'?

SUSAN. But of course! What a good idea——

LINDA. Mary asked if—— I'll have a bag packed. *(*JULIA *comes in.)* Oh, hello, dear.—Are you back already?

JULIA. Isn't it late? Hello, Susan. Hello, Nick. I thought you were sailing. *(She leaves her evening wrap on the sofa, Left, and moves toward the writing table at Right.)*

SUSAN. We are.

NICK. At the crack of twelve. On the way now, in fact.

JULIA. I hope you have a grand trip.

SUSAN. Thanks. *(*DELIA *enters and takes* JULIA's *wrap from the sofa.)*

LINDA. —Delia, will you pack a bag for me, please? I'm going to Mrs. Hedges until Tuesday.

DELIA. Yes, Miss. *(She goes out.* NICK *and* SUSAN *stand at Center, facing* JULIA.*)*

SUSAN. I'm sorry we won't be here for the wedding, Julia.

JULIA. I'm sorry too, Susan.

NICK. When's it to be?

JULIA. We haven't quite—set a date, yet.

SUSAN. —In the Spring, some time?

JULIA. Possibly before.

NICK. Let us know, won't you?

JULIA. Of course.

NICK. *(A brief pause. Then)* —Then you're not coming down to the boat tonight?

JULIA. I'm afraid I can't. Bon voyage, though.

NICK. *(Thinks rapidly)* Thanks. Can we take any word to Johnny for you?

JULIA. To Johnny?

NICK. Yes.—Or a basket of fruit, maybe?

JULIA. He'll be there, will he?

NICK. *(This, at any rate,* NICK *can do)* I should imagine so, if he's sailing.

JULIA. Sailing!

NICK. Isn't he?

JULIA. I wasn't aware of it.

NICK. Well, all I know is that the morning he left for wherever he went to, he telephoned me to get him a single cabin through Andrews, of the French Line. I don't believe it's been given up, or I'd have heard from them. I thought of course you knew, or I——

JULIA. I think I should—if he were going.

NICK. Yes, I suppose so. *(To* SUSAN*)* We won't expect him, then.

SUSAN. No.—Goodbye, Julia. *(They move together toward the door.)*

NICK. Look us up, when you arrive. Immigrant's Bank.—We'll see you later, Linda.

LINDA. I'll be ready.

SUSAN. Thanks. Lovely evening——

NICK and SUSAN. *(Together)* —And you must come and see *us* some time! *(They go out. There is a silence.* JULIA *looks for a cigarette.)*

LINDA. It may be true, Julia. I think the chances are it is.

JULIA. What?

LINDA. —That Johnny's going with them.

JULIA. *(Laughs)* Not possibly, darling!—Why don't they keep these cigarette boxes filled——

LINDA. Stop it, Julia!

JULIA. Stop it?

LINDA. —Pretending you don't give a damn.

JULIA. *(Finds and lights a cigarette)* You seem to be taking my little difficulty more seriously than I am. *(She moves toward the sofa at Left.)*

LINDA. If you don't want Johnny to go off to-night and make a hash of both your lives, you'd better send him some word to the boat.

JULIA. *(Smiles)* Somehow, I don't think that's necessary.

LINDA. Why not?

JULIA. Well, for one reason, because he won't be there. He's no more sailing tonight than I am.

LINDA. You don't know that he's not!

JULIA. I don't know that he is, so I think I'm safe in assuming it.—Do you want to go to the Todds' dinner on Wednesday? They telephoned—

LINDA. —Julia, why do you want to shut me out in the cold like this?

JULIA. I wasn't aware that I was.

LINDA. —But won't you just *talk* to me! Oh, please, Julia——

JULIA. I don't know what there is to say.

LINDA. Never so long as I remember has there been anything we couldn't——

JULIA. If there's been any shutting out done, it's you who've done it, Linda.

LINDA. Me?!

JULIA. Johnny and I have had a difference of opinion, and you're siding with him, aren't you?

LINDA. But he's right! He's right for you as well as for himself——

JULIA. I think that's for me to decide.

LINDA. Not Father?

JULIA. Father has nothing to do with it——

LINDA. Oh, no!

JULIA. He happens to agree with me where you don't, that's all.

LINDA. We've always agreed before—always.

JULIA. No—I think quite often I've given in, in order to avoid scenes and upsets and—oh, well——

LINDA. *(A silence. Then)* —Is that true, Julia?

JULIA. You've always been the "stronger character," haven't you? At least people have always thought so. You've made all the decisions, you've always had the ideas——

LINDA. —And you've been resenting me right from the very—— *(She moves away from her, toward the fireplace)* Oh—I can't believe it——

JULIA. It's nothing to get in a state about—and I didn't say I resented you. You've been an immense help, often. But when it comes to determining my future, and the future of the man I'm going to marry——

LINDA. *(Turns on her sharply)* —Your future! What do you want, Julia—just security? Sit back in your feather-boa among the Worthies of the World?

JULIA. Well, I'm certain that one thing I *don't* want is to start this endless, aimless discussion all over again.

LINDA. But I tell you you can't *stand* this sort of life forever—not if you're the person I think you are. And when it starts going thin on you, what'll you have to hold on to?—Lois Evans shot herself —why? Franny Grant's up the Hudson in a sanitarium—why?

JULIA. I'm sure I don't know.

LINDA. —Nothing left to do or have or want— that's why—and no insides! There's not a poor girl in town who isn't happier than we are—at least they still *want* what we've got—*they* think it's good. *(She turns away)* —If they knew!

JULIA. —And *I* think it's good.

LINDA. Lord, Julia, don't tell me that you *want* it!

JULIA. I want it, and it's all I want.

LINDA. *(There is a silence. Then)* —Then it's goodbye, Julia.

JULIA. Oh, Linda, for Heaven's sake don't be so ridiculous! If you're so damn set on being violent, get a few Russians in and talk life with a great big L to them.

EDWARD. *(Comes in, an admonishing finger raised)* Ah—ah—ah!

LINDA. *(Turns to him)* —Father, I think you're both giving Johnny the rottenest kind of a deal.

EDWARD. In what way?

LINDA. Every way! Why do you do it? It can't be that you think he's out to marry for money. You must realize how simple it would have been for him —to conform to specifications now, and then just not get up some fine morning.

EDWARD. *(Moves to the table behind the sofa at Right)* I don't regard the young man as a fortune-hunter, Linda.

LINDA. Well, what is it, then?

EDWARD. *(Finds a cigarette and comes forward*

with it) —I think his outlook has merely become— somewhat confused, shall we say, and——

LINDA. —And you'll straighten it out for him.

EDWARD. *(To* JULIA*)* We shall try, shan't we, daughter?

LINDA. Why hasn't he a right to spend some part of his life as he wants to? He can afford it. What's he got to do? Pile up so much that he can be comfortable on the income of his income?

EDWARD. *(Seats himself in a chair near the sofa)* —That would be an excellent aim, but I think we shall hardly require it of him.

LINDA. I'd like to hear the requirements.

EDWARD. Any self-respecting young man wishes to earn enough to support his wife and his family.

LINDA. Even when his wife already has——? Even when there's no possible need of it?

EDWARD. Even then.

LINDA. Oh, Father, what a fake idea that is!

EDWARD. I don't think so. Nor does Julia.—In addition, he has somehow developed a very curious attitude toward work——

LINDA. It seems to me saner than most. He wants his leisure at this end—good sense, I call it. —Which is harder to do, anyway——? Go to an office and rustle papers about or sit under a tree and look at your own soul?

JULIA. *(Contemptuously)* Heavens!—The office, I should say.

LINDA. Then you've never looked, Julia.

JULIA. You can't talk to her, Father.

EDWARD. I should like to understand what he— and you—are aiming at, Linda, but I must confess I cannot. (NED *comes in.)* —I consider his whole attitude deliberately un-American.

LINDA. *(Stares at* EDWARD*)* Are you serious?

EDWARD. Entirely.

LINDA. *(She stares for a moment more)* —You're right. I believe it is.

NED. *(Seats himself on the sofa, at Left)* I've always said the Americans were a great little people.

LINDA. —Then he's a bad one, and will go to hell when he dies. Because apparently he can't quite believe that a life devoted to piling up money is all it's cracked up to be.—That's strange, isn't it—when he has us, right before his eyes, for such a shining example?

JULIA. I thought *you* were the one who found leisure so empty.

LINDA. —You think I call this, leisure? A life-sentence to *this?*—Or that he does?

JULIA. I think any variety of it he'd find quite as empty.

LINDA. —Even if it should be, he's got a right to discover it for himself! Can't you see that?

JULIA. I can see the discovery would come, quick enough.

LINDA. —And you don't want to be with him to lend a hand, if it should? *(JULIA is silent.)*

EDWARD. Linda, I listened most attentively to our young dreamer the other day. I have listened quite as attentively to you this evening. I am not entirely without intelligence, but I must still confess that most of your talk seems to me to be of the seventeen-year-old variety.

LINDA. I'm glad if it is! We're all grand at seventeen. It's after that that the—sickness sets in.

EDWARD. *(Chuckles, shakes his head and rises)* —I feel very well, myself—and you look in perfect health, my dear. *(He moves toward the door.)*

LINDA. —You both think he'll come around, Father—compromise, anyway. You'll get fooled. He won't give way one little inch.

EDWARD *(At the door* EDWARD *turns, smiling)* Stubborn—?

LINDA. Right! And sure he's right!

EDWARD. We shall see—— *(He goes out, victor.)*

JULIA. —Is that all, Linda?

LINDA. Where are you going?

JULIA. To bed.

LINDA. Now?

JULIA. Yes. Have you any objections?

LINDA. You actually won't lift a finger to keep him off that boat tonight?

JULIA. He has no idea of taking it.

LINDA. You don't know him!

JULIA. Well, I think I know him a little better than you. I happen to be engaged to him.

(HENRY has entered with a tray containing a decanter of whisky, ice, a bottle of soda, and one glass.)

NED. Thanks, Henry. *(HENRY bows and goes out.)*

JULIA. Ned, I thought you went to the theatre with the Wheelers——

NED. I did, but it was so bad I left. *(He rises, goes behind the table and makes himself a drink.)*

JULIA. Wasn't that just a trifle rude?

NED. I don't know, Julia. Look it up under R in the book of etiquette, will you?

JULIA. I can't imagine what you're thinking of these days.—Drinking alone—that's pretty too, isn't it?

NED. I never thought of the aesthetic side, but I see what you mean. *(He takes a long swallow of his drink.)*

JULIA. *(Regards him contemptuously, then, to* LINDA*)* If there's any message of any sort, I wish you'd ring my room.

LINDA. All right. (JULIA *goes out.* LINDA *seats herself and stares moodily in front of her.)*

NED. —Like a drink?

LINDA. No, thanks.

NED. *(Again settles down upon the sofa)* —You know, most people, including Johnny and yourself, make a big mistake about Julia.

LINDA. What's that?

NED. They're taken in by her looks. At bottom she's a very dull girl, and the life she pictures for herself is the life she belongs in. *(The TELE-PHONE rings.* LINDA *goes to it.)*

LINDA. —You've never hit it off, that's all. *(At the telephone)* Hello.—Yes.—Yes.—What? When, do you know?—Well, ask, will you? *(To* NED*)* He *was* there.

NED. Who and where?

LINDA. Johnny—Placid. *(To the telephone)* Yes? This—? I see. No. No. That's right. Thanks. *(She puts down the telephone and turns again to* NED*)* —And left this noon.

NED. Then he'll be around tonight.

LINDA. You think so? This late?

NED. He'll be around.

LINDA. *(A moment. Then)* Ned——

NED. What?

LINDA. Do you remember what we talked about New Year's Eve?

NED. *(A brief pause. Then)* Sure—I remember

LINDA. Tell me something——

NED. Sure.

LINDA. Does it stand out all over me?

NED. Why?

LINDA. Nick and Susan—I think they got it.

NED. Anyone who loves you would, Linda.

LINDA. Oh, that's awful. I'm so ashamed—— *(Then she raises her head)* I'm not. though!

NED. Why should you be?

LINDA. *(Suddenly)* Look here, Ned—you're in a jam too, aren't you?

NED. Me?

LINDA. You.

NED. Sure, I suppose so.

LINDA. Is it that you hate this—— *(Her gesture includes the house and all it represents)* —Or that you love that—— *(She indicates his drink.)*

NED. H'm—— *(He looks about him)* Well, God knows I hate all this—— *(And lifts the glass before his eyes)* —And God knows I'm crazy mad over this—— *(He takes a deep swallow and sets the glass down)* I guess it's both.

LINDA. What are we going to do?

NED. Nothing, that I know of.

LINDA. But we must!

NED. *(Hunches down into the sofa)* I'm all right.

LINDA. You're not—but you'll pull out of it—and *I'll* pull out of it.

NED. I'm all right. I don't mind any more.

LINDA. You've got to mind. We can't just let go, can we?

NED. *I* can. I have.

LINDA. No. No!

NED. Listen, Linda: I've had the whole thing out with myself, see? All of it. A lot of times. And I've developed my what-do-you-call-it—technique. I'm all right. There's no reason for stewing over me. I'm—*(He squints at his glass)* —very happy.

LINDA. There must be some sort of life for you—

NED. —But there *is!* Haven't I got the swell Seton name to uphold? *(He laughs shortly)* —Only that's where I'll fox it. I'll make *it* uphold me.

LINDA. Neddy—listen: After the wedding we'll go out to Boulder, both of us.—We'll live on horseback and in trout streams all day long every day until we're in hand again. We'll get so damn tired that we won't be able to want anything or think of anything but sleep.

NED. You make it too hard. Come on—have a drink——

LINDA. Oh, you're dying, Neddy!

NED. *(Very patiently)* All right, Linda.

LINDA. Won't you do that with me?

NED. Thanks, but uh-uh. Nope.

LINDA. *(Moves away from him to the other side of the room)* Oh, won't anyone ever again do what I *know* they should do?

NED. That's what's the matter with you, Linda. You worry so much over other people's troubles you don't get anywhere with your own. (HENRY *enters.* LINDA *is staring at* NED.)

HENRY. —Mr. Case, Miss.

LINDA. *(A silence, then* LINDA *recovers herself)* Yes?—Have him come up, will you? (HENRY *bows and goes out. A moment.* NED *watches her. Then:)*

NED. —Are you sure you *want* to get over him?

LINDA. No. I'm not. And that's what scares me most. I feel alive, and I love it. I feel at last something's happening to me. But it can't get anywhere, so it's like living on—*your* stuff. I've *got* to get over it.

NED. —Because it seems so hopeless, is that it?

LINDA. Seems! What do you mean?

NED. Don't you know? (LINDA *can only look at him. He goes to her)* —Then let me tell you something: you're twice as attractive as Julia ever thought of being. You've got twice the looks, and twice the mind, and ten times the guts. You've lived in her shade for years now, and there's nothing to it. You could charm a bird off a tree, if you would. And why not? If you were in her way, she'd ride you down like a rabbit.

LINDA. *(Softly)* Oh, you stinker—knowing the way she loves him—you stinker, Ned.

NED. *(Shrugs)* All right. *(He wanders in the direction of the door)* —Tell him Hello for me, will you?

LINDA. (LINDA's *voice rises*) —If there's one thing I'll do in my life, it'll be to let the fresh air back into you again, hear me?—I'll do it if I have to shoot you.

NED. *(Turns and smiles back at her)* —All right. *(He goes out. With an exclamation* LINDA *goes to the window and looks out, huddling herself in her arms.)*

JOHNNY. *(Enters. A moment, then)* Hello, Linda.

LINDA. Hello, Johnny.

JOHNNY. Is——? (LINDA *moves to the telephone.)*

LINDA. I'll send for her.

JOHNNY. Wait a minute. *(A silence. He looks about him)* I feel as if I'd—been away quite a while.

LINDA. Yes.

JOHNNY. I went to Placid.

LINDA. I see.

JOHNNY. It was horrible there.

LINDA. I can imagine it.

JOHNNY. Oh, Linda, I love her so——

LINDA. Of course you do, Johnny.

JOHNNY. It—makes anything else—any plans—ideas—anything——

LINDA. —Seem so unimportant, of course.

JOHNNY. But I know they are important! I know that!

LINDA. *(Smiles)* Still——

JOHNNY. *(Turns away)* That's it—*still*——

LINDA. *(A moment)* I think it'll come out all right, Johnny.

JOHNNY. Maybe, in the long run.

LINDA. Have you—I suppose you've decided something or other——

JOHNNY. I'm going to stay at my job, if that's what you mean.

LINDA. *(After a moment, very quietly)* I see.

JOHNNY. But only for a while! Only a couple of years, say—just until I can get through to her that —well, it's what she asked, and after all, a couple of years isn't a lifetime.

LINDA. No, of course not.

JOHNNY. I can see the way they look at it—I could hardly expect them suddenly to do a complete about-face, and—but hang it, they ought at least to see what I'm getting at!

LINDA. Perhaps eventually they will.

JOHNNY. That's what I'm counting on.

LINDA. *(Another silence. Then)* The fun's gone out of you, Johnny. That's too bad.

JOHNNY. *(Stares at the floor)* It'll be back.

LINDA. I hope.

JOHNNY. *(Looks up suddenly)* Linda—you agree that there's only the one thing for me to do now—

LINDA. *(Smiles again)* Compromise——

JOHNNY. Yes, damn it! But *you* think that's right, don't you?

LINDA. I don't think it matters a bit what I think——

JOHNNY. *(Goes to her suddenly and seizes her wrists)* It does, though! You think it's right, don't you? Say you think it's right!

LINDA. Shall I send for Julia?

JOHNNY. Say it first!

LINDA. *(With difficulty)* Johnny—when two people love each other as much as you, anything that keeps them apart must be wrong.—Will that do? (JOHNNY *drops her hand and moves away from her.)* —And shall I send for her now?

JOHNNY. Go ahead.

LINDA. *(Goes to the telephone and presses a button in the box beside it)* With luck, we'll manage not to include Father this time.

JOHNNY. Oh, Lord, yes! (LINDA *again presses the button, and again several times.)* Asleep, probably——

LINDA. Of course not. *(She presses it again. Then)* Julia—yes—would you come down a minute? No—but there's no telegram *to* send up. Will you come, Julia? *(Her voice changes)* Julia, it's terribly important that you come down here at once. *(She replaces the telephone and turns to* JOHNNY*)* She'll be right down.

JOHNNY. If she doesn't fall asleep again.

LINDA. Johnny—don't talk like that. I can't stand to hear your voice do that.

JOHNNY. You care more what happens to me than she does.

LINDA. *(Startled)* What? Don't be silly. *(Then, with difficulty)* Maybe I feel things about you that she doesn't because—well, maybe just because *I'm* not in love with you.

JOHNNY. You know what I think of you, don't you?

LINDA. *(Smiles)* I'd be glad to hear.

JOHNNY. I like you better than anyone else in the world.

LINDA. That's very nice, Johnny—because I like you a good deal, too. *(For a long moment their eyes hold them together. Then* EDWARD *comes in and, with a start,* LINDA *sees him)* Oh, for the love of Pete——

EDWARD. *(Advances to* JOHNNY, *hand outstretched)* Well, well—good evening!

JOHNNY. Good evening, sir. *(They shake hands.)*

LINDA. *(Turns away.)* —Both members of this club.

EDWARD. They tell me you've been away. Very pleasant, having you back.

JOHNNY. It's pleasant to be back.

EDWARD. —Quite at the mercy of the snow these days, aren't we?

JOHNNY. Quite.

EDWARD. *(Moves toward the fireplace)* Still, they say Americans need four seasons, so I suppose we oughtn't to complain, eh?

JOHNNY. I suppose not.

LINDA. Father—Johnny came tonight to see Julia——

EDWARD. —That doesn't surprise me a great deal, Daughter—not a great deal!

LINDA. —Julia—not you and me.—Come on—let's go byebye.

JULIA. *(Enters)* Linda, what's the idea of——? *(She sees JOHNNY)* Oh——

JOHNNY. *(Goes to her swiftly)* Get a wrap, will you? We're going out——

JULIA. *(Hesitates)* Father—you won't mind if Johnny and I——

EDWARD. Please close the door. I wish to speak with both of you. *(JULIA gestures helplessly to JOHNNY and closes the door.)* —You insist upon putting me in a position that I don't in the least relish—— *(JULIA seats herself upon the bench at Left. The door is opened again, tentatively.)* Who's that?—Oh, come in, Ned, come in.

NED. *(Enters and moves toward his drink)* Sorry.—I just wanted——

EDWARD. Sit down, Son—— *(NED seats himself upon the sofa Left. EDWARD continues to JULIA and JOHNNY)* —Coming between two young people in love is furthest from my wish and intention.—Love, true love, is a very rare and beautiful thing, and— *(NED rises and moves silently toward the door.)* Where are you going? Please sit down! *(He waits*

until NED *has returned to his place, then continues)*
—And I believe its path—that is to say, the path of
true love, contrary to the adage, *should* run smooth.
But in order that it may—I am a man of fifty-eight
years, and speak from a long experience and obser-
vation—it is of paramount importance that——

JOHNNY. I beg your pardon, sir.

EDWARD. Yes?

JOHNNY. If Pritchard, Ames still want me, I'll
go with them when we get back from our wedding-
trip—about March first, say. (LINDA *turns away.
There is a silence. Then:)*

JULIA. *(Softly)* Oh, Johnny—— *(She goes to
him.)*

JOHNNY. I'm still not convinced—I still don't believe in it, but it's what Julia wishes and—and I'm
—glad to defer to her wish.

LINDA. And now, in Heaven's name, may they be
left alone—or shall we all move over to Madison
Square Garden?

EDWARD. *(Disregarding her)* You are not convinced, you say—— (LINDA *exclaims impatiently.)*

JOHNNY. Would you like me to lie to you, sir?

JULIA. It's enough for me, Father.

JOHNNY. Julia said a year or two. I'll stay with
them three years. I'll work harder than ever I've
worked before. I'll do everything I can to make a
success of it. I only ask that if at the end of the
three years I still feel that it's wise to quit for a
while, there won't be any more objections.

EDWARD. I doubt if by that time there'll be reason for any.

JOHNNY. We'll have to see about that, sir.

JULIA. Well, Father?

EDWARD. *(A pause. Then)* When is it you wish
to be married?

JULIA. As soon as possible.

JOHNNY. Sooner.

EDWARD. The invitations must be out for ten days at least.—How would two weeks from Wednesday suit you?

JULIA. That would be perfect.

EDWARD. No doubt there will be a sailing later that week.—Well, now, the sun's shining once more, isn't it?—And we're all friends again, eh?

LINDA. Just one big family.

EDWARD. —And what are your plans for your wedding-trip, may I ask?

JOHNNY. We haven't any very definite ones. Mostly France, I expect.

EDWARD. It's well to arrange even honeymoons a bit in advance.—Now let me suggest a little itinerary: You'll land at Plymouth or Southampton, and proceed straight to London. I'll cable my sister to-morrow. She and her husband will be delighted to have you stay with them.

LINDA. Good Lord, Father——

EDWARD. (To JOHNNY) He is Sir Horace Porter—one of the most important men in British banking circles.

JULIA. Father, I'm not sure——

EDWARD. You can scarcely go abroad and not stop with your Aunt Helen, Julia. In addition, it will save hotel expense and Johnny will be able to learn something of British methods.—Then I shall cable the Bouviers in Paris.—He was expert adviser to the Minister of Finance in the late war—a very good man for you to know. If they aren't already in Cannes, they will be very glad to have you visit them. And if they are, you could not do better than go straight to the South yourselves and——

JOHNNY. I had thought of this as more of a lark than a business trip, sir.

EDWARD. —But there's no harm in combining a little business with pleasure, is there? I've never found there was.

JULIA. *(To* JOHNNY*)* They have a lovely place in Cannes.

EDWARD. A week in London—a week in Paris—

LINDA. An hour in the Louvre——

EDWARD. —Ten days in Cannes—ideal! Then you might sail from Genoa and return by the Southern route. *(To* JULIA*)* I'll arrange to have your house ready for you to go into March first.

JULIA. —Thanks, dear.

JOHNNY. What house is that, Julia?

JULIA. Father's lending us the sweetest little place on Sixty-fourth Street.

NED. *(To* LINDA*)* Would you call the Sixty-fourth Street house little?

LINDA. *(Watching* JOHNNY*)* —By comparison.

EDWARD. *(To* JULIA*)* And I have also decided to turn the cottage at The Poplars over to you for the summers.

JULIA. Father, you shouldn't—you really should not! *(She goes to him and takes his hand.)*

NED. Now there *is* a small place—hasn't even got a ballroom.

JULIA. Oh, Johnny—wait till you see it!

EDWARD. *(Is beaming)* This is not a deed of gift, you know—not yet. Perhaps when you have occupied them for—er—five years or so, my hard old heart may soften.

JULIA. —Listen to him—*his* hard old heart! *(To* JOHNNY*)* —Have you ever known of anyone so sweet?

JOHNNY. *(After a moment)* Julia—I'm sorry—but I can't stand it.

JULIA. *(A silence. Then)* Would you—mind telling me what you mean?

JOHNNY. If we begin loaded down with possessions, obligations, responsibilities, how would we ever get out from under them? We never would.

EDWARD. Ah?

JOHNNY. —No. You're extremely generous—and kind—but it's not for me.

EDWARD. And may I ask what *is* for you?

JOHNNY. I don't know yet, but I do know it's not this.

EDWARD. *(Very quietly)* We are to understand, then, that you are *not* returning to work.

JOHNNY. That work? For this? *(He shakes his head)* —No.

JULIA. But you said—!

JOHNNY. —I'm back where I was, now. I can see now that it's got to be a clean break, it's simply got to.

EDWARD. But the other day, if I remember correctly, you intimated that you might follow some occupation——

JOHNNY. Eventually, yes. I think I may still be fairly active at thirty-five or forty.

EDWARD. —And in the meantime you expect just to lie fallow, is that it?

JOHNNY. Not lie—be! I expect to dig and plow and water for all I'm worth.

EDWARD. Toward the—er—eventual occupation which is to overtake you——

JOHNNY. Exactly.

EDWARD. I see.—Julia, if you marry this young man now, I doubt if he will ever again earn one penny. *(He moves to the table behind the sofa, at Right.)*

JOHNNY. *(Advances)* Julia, if it's important to you, I'll promise you I shall always earn my own living. And what's more, if there's need of it, I'll always earn yours.

JULIA. Thanks.

JOHNNY. Oh, my dear, we've got to make our own life—there's nothing to it if we don't—there's no other way to live it!—Let's forget wedding invitations and two weeks from Wednesday. Let's go now. Let's be married tonight. (EDWARD *turns, in amazement.*)

JULIA. I must decide now, must I?

JOHNNY. Please——

JULIA. —And if I say No—not unless you——?

JOHNNY. —Then I'm going tonight, by myself.

JULIA. *(A moment. Then)* Very well—you can go. Because I don't quite see myself with an idler for a husband.

JOHNNY. *(A silence. Then* JOHNNY *speaks slowly)* I suppose the fact is, I love feeling free inside even better than I love you, Julia.

JULIA. Apparently—or what you call feeling free.

JOHNNY. *(Turns to* EDWARD*)* Goodbye, sir. I'm sorry we couldn't make a go of it. Thanks for trying, anyhow. *(He goes to* LINDA *and takes both her hands)* —Goodbye to you, Linda. You've been sweet.

LINDA. Goodbye, Johnny. So have you.—I hope you find what you're looking for.

JOHNNY. I hope *you* do.

LINDA. You did want someone along with you on the big search, didn't you?

JOHNNY. I did, you know.

LINDA. Poor boy.

JOHNNY. —But we won't mind, will we?

LINDA. Hell, no—*we* won't mind.

JOHNNY. We'll get there——

LINDA. Sure! *We'll* get there!

JOHNNY. Linda——

LINDA. *(She leans toward him)* Oh, please do—

JOHNNY. *(Bends, kisses her briefly, and moves toward the door)* Goodbye, Ned. (NED *attempts a goodbye, but cannot say it.* JOHNNY *goes out. There is a complete silence for a moment. Then* LINDA *murmurs:)*

LINDA. I'll miss that man. *(Another silence, which* JULIA *finally breaks:)*

JULIA. *(Half to herself)* —He's really gone, then.

EDWARD. Yes.—And in my opinion——

LINDA. *(Turns sharply)* —Good riddance, eh? *(*EDWARD *nods sagely.)*

JULIA. —Really gone——

LINDA. *(Goes to her)* —Oh, never mind, dear, never mind. If he loves you, he'll be back!

JULIA. *(Turns upon her)* —Be back? Be *back*, did you say? What do you think I am? Do you think all I've got to do with my time is to persuade a—a lightweight like him that there's something to life but having fun and more fun? *(*LINDA *stares, unable to speak.)*

EDWARD. I hope, Julia, that this experience, hard as it may have been, will teach you that——

JULIA. Oh, don't worry about me! I'm all right. *(She laughs briefly)* —Even a little more than all right, I should say.

NED. *(Rises)* —Um.—Narrow squeak, wasn't it? *(Suddenly* LINDA *grasps* JULIA'S *arm.)*

JULIA. What's the matter with you?

LINDA. You don't love him.

JULIA. Will you kindly let go my arm?

LINDA. You don't love him!

JULIA. Will you *please*——

LINDA. Answer me! Do you or do you not?

JULIA. And what's that to you, may I ask?

EDWARD. Now, children——

LINDA. What's it to me! Oh, what's it to me! *(Her grasp tightens on* JULIA'S *arm)* Answer me!

JULIA. Father—what's the matter with her?

LINDA. You don't, do you? I can *see* you don't. It's written all over you. You're relieved he's gone —*relieved!*

JULIA. And suppose I am?

LINDA. —She asks me suppose she is! *(Again she confronts* JULIA*)* Are you? Say it!

JULIA. *(Wrenches herself free)* —I'm so relieved I could sing with it.—Is that what you want?

LINDA. Yes!—Thanks! *(She throws back her head and laughs with joy, and moves quickly to the table behind the sofa at Left)* Oh, Lordy, Lordy —have I got a job now! *(From her handbag on the table she takes two brown envelopes, goes to NED and gives him one of them)*

NED. What is it? *(He sees)* Passport——

LINDA. What do you say?

NED. When?

LINDA. Now. Tonight.

NED. Oh, I couldn't tonight.

LINDA. Of course you could! If I can, you can.

EDWARD. *(Advances)* Linda, where are you off to?

LINDA. *(To NED)* Will you come?

NED. Well, you know I'd like to, but——

LINDA. Then come!

EDWARD. Linda, where are you going? Tell me instantly.

LINDA. —On a trip. On a big ride. Oh, what a ride! Do you mind?

NED. Listen, Father, I'd——

EDWARD. A trip now is out of the question. Please remember you have a position to fill. You are not an idler. *(To LINDA)* —A trip where?

LINDA. *(To NED)* You won't?

NED. I can't.

LINDA. —Caught.

NED. Maybe.

LINDA. —I'll be back for you, Ned.

NED. *(Almost inaudibly)* I'll—be here——

DELIA. *(Enters)* Excuse me, Miss Linda—Mr. and Mrs. Potter are waiting in the car. Your bag has gone down.

LINDA. Bring my fur coat, will you, Delia?—And

throw a couple of hats in the hatbox and take it down, too.

DELIA. Very well, Miss. (DELIA *goes out.)*

LINDA. *(Turns to* JULIA*)* —You've got no faith in Johnny, have you, Julia? His little dream may fall flat, you think—yes! So it may! What about it? What if it should? There'll be another—the point is, he *does* dream! Oh, I've got all the faith in the world in Johnny. Whatever he does is all right with me. If he wants to sit on his tail, he can sit on his tail. If he wants to come back and sell peanuts, Lord how I'll believe in those peanuts!— Goodbye, Julia.—Goodbye, Father. *(She leaves them and goes to* NED*)* Goodbye, Neddy——

(Warn CURTAIN.)

NED. Goodbye, kid—good luck—— *(For a moment they cling together. Then:)*

LINDA. Oh, never you fear, I'll be back for you, my fine bucko!

NED. All right, kid. *(She moves toward the door.* NED *is drawn after her.* DELIA *enters with the fur coat.* LINDA *takes it from her.* DELIA *goes out.)*

EDWARD. As yet you have not said where it is you are——

JULIA. *(Exclaims suddenly)* I know!

LINDA. *(Going out)* —And try to stop me, some-one! Oh, please—someone try to stop me! *(She is gone.)*

NED. *(Stands looking after her, murmuring soft-ly)* Oh, God, oh, God——

EDWARD. I shall not permit it! I shall——

NED. —Permit it!—Permit Linda?—Don't make me laugh, Father.

JULIA. *(Advancing)* She's going *with* them, isn't she? *Isn't* she?

NED. *(Smiles and picks up his glass again)* —Going to get her Johnny.

JULIA. *(Laughs shortly)* A fine chance she's got!

NED. —Any bets? *(Then savagely)* —Any bets, Julia? *(He raises his glass)* —To Linda—— *(The portrait above the fireplace catches his eye)* —And while we're at it—Grandfather! *(He drinks.)*

CURTAIN

"HOLIDAY"

PROPERTY PLOT

ACT I

Magazines.
Newspapers.
Cigarette box.
Writing material.
Ashtray.
Tray (CHARLES).
Lucky Strike cigarettes (JOHNNY).
Lighter (JOHNNY).

ACT II

Toys.
Music-box.
Gramophone.
2 whisky and sodas (NED).
Linen, silver, plates, glasses on tray (HENRY).
2 bottles champagne in pail (CHARLES).
Plate of sandwiches (CHARLES).
Chafing dish (HENRY).
Cold meats on platter (CHARLES).

ACT III

Coffee service.
Cigarettes.
Whisky, ice, soda, glass on tray (HENRY).
2 brown envelopes (LINDA's bag).

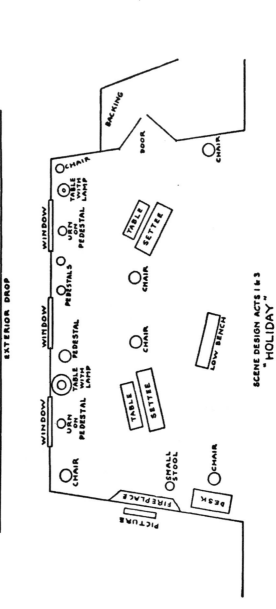

SCENE DESIGN ACTS 1 & 3
"HOLIDAY"

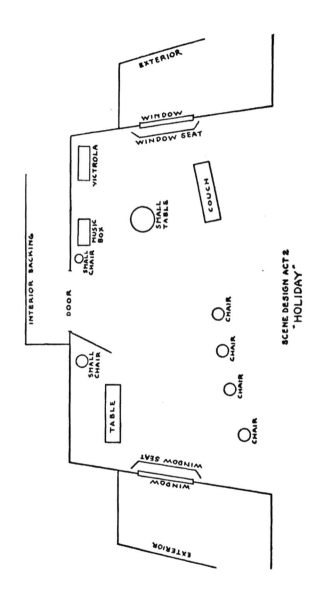

SCENE DESIGN ACT 2
"HOLIDAY"

Also By
Philip Barry

THE ANIMAL KINGDOM

FOOLISH NOTION

HERE COME THE CLOWNS

HOTEL UNIVERSE

IN A GARDEN

JADE GOD

LIBERTY JONES

PARIS BOUND

THE PHILADELPHIA STORY

SPRING DANCE

TOMORROW AND TOMORROW

THE YOUNGEST

YOU AND I

Please visit our website **samuelfrench.com** for complete
descriptions and licensing information

OTHER TITLES AVAILABLE FROM SAMUEL FRENCH

THE PHILADELPHIA STORY
Philip Barry

Comedy / 9m, 6f / Interior, Exterior
This Broadway hit starred Katharine Hepburn as Tracy Lord of the
Philadelphia Lords, an inhibited and spoiled daughter of the privi-
leged. Divorced from C.J. Dexter Haven, she is engaged to a successful young snob. A gossip weekly sends a reporter and a camera
woman to report the wedding arrangements and they are injected
into the house by Tracy's brother who hopes to divert their attention
from father's romance with a Broadway dancer. Tracy finds herself
growing interested in Connor, the fascinating reporter. At the end
of a pre wedding party, Tracy and Connor take a moonlight dip in
the pool and meet her ex husband and finance on their way back to
the house. The following morning her intended agrees to forgive
her, but his smug attitude enrages Tracy and she breaks off the engagement. Connor offers to marry her, but she turns him down and
remarries Dexter, to the satisfaction of everyone.

SAMUEL FRENCH STAFF

Nate Collins
President

Ken Dingledine
Director of Operations,
Vice President

Bruce Lazarus
Executive Director,
General Counsel

Rita Maté
Director of Finance

ACCOUNTING

Lori Thimsen | Director of Licensing Compliance
Nehal Kumar | Senior Accounting Associate
Josephine Messina | Accounts Payable
Helena Mezzina | Royalty Administration
Joe Garner | Royalty Administration
Jessica Zheng | Accounts Receivable
Andy Lian | Accounts Receivable
Zoe Qiu | Accounts Receivable
Charlie Sou | Accounting Associate
Joann Mannello | Orders Administrator

BUSINESS AFFAIRS

Lysna Marzani | Director of Business Affairs
Kathryn McCumber | Business Administrator

CUSTOMER SERVICE AND LICENSING

Brad Lohrenz | Director of Licensing Development
Fred Schnitzer | Business Development Manager
Laura Lindson | Licensing Services Manager
Kim Rogers | Professional Licensing Associate
Matthew Akers | Amateur Licensing Associate
Ashley Byrne | Amateur Licensing Associate
Glenn Halcomb | Amateur Licensing Associate
Derek Hassler | Amateur Licensing Associate
Jennifer Carter | Amateur Licensing Associate
Kelly McCready | Amateur Licensing Associate
Annette Storckman | Amateur Licensing Associate
Chris Lonstrup | Outgoing Information Specialist

EDITORIAL AND PUBLICATIONS

Amy Rose Marsh | Literary Manager
Ben Coleman | Editorial Associate
Gene Sweeney | Graphic Designer
David Geer | Publications Supervisor
Charlyn Brea | Publications Associate
Tyler Mullen | Publications Associate

MARKETING

Abbie Van Nostrand | Director of Corporate
Communications
Ryan Pointer | Marketing Manager
Courtney Kochuba | Marketing Associate

OPERATIONS

Joe Ferreira | Product Development Manager
Casey McLain | Operations Supervisor
Danielle Heckman | Office Coordinator, Reception

SAMUEL FRENCH BOOKSHOP (LOS ANGELES)

Joyce Mehess | Bookstore Manager
Cory DeLair | Bookstore Buyer
Jennifer Palumbo | Customer Service Associate
Sonya Wallace | Bookstore Associate
Tim Coultas | Bookstore Associate
Monté Patterson | Bookstore Associate
Robin Hushbeck | Bookstore Associate
Alfred Contreras | Shipping & Receiving

LONDON OFFICE

Felicity Barks | Rights & Contracts Associate
Steve Blacker | Bookshop Associate
David Bray | Customer Services Associate
Zena Choi | Professional Licensing Associate
Robert Cooke | Assistant Buyer
Stephanie Dawson | Amateur Licensing Associate
Simon Ellison | Retail Sales Manager
Jason Felix | Royalty Administration
Susan Griffiths | Amateur Licensing Associate
Robert Hamilton | Amateur Licensing Associate
Lucy Hume | Publications Manager
Nasir Khan | Management Accountant
Simon Magniti | Royalty Administration
Louise Mappley | Amateur Licensing Associate
James Nicolau | Despatch Associate
Martin Phillips | Librarian
Zubayed Rahman | Despatch Associate
Steve Sanderson | Royalty Administration Supervisor
Douglas Schatz | Acting Executive Director
Roger Sheppard | I.T. Manager
Geoffrey Skinner | Company Accountant
Peter Smith | Amateur Licensing Associate
Garry Spratley | Customer Service Manager
David Webster | UK Operations Director